Vivian S. Rossetti

Training for Successful INVALSI

Quaderno di allenamento alla Prova Nazionale di inglese

per la
Scuola Secondaria di Secondo Grado

Coordinamento editoriale: **Paola Maletto**
Redazione e impaginazione: **Fregi e Majuscole s.r.l.**
Progetto grafico: **Tatiana Fragni**
Copertina: **Elena Petruccelli**
Immagine di copertina: **Shutterstock**: Pablo Calvog
Controllo qualità: **Andrea Mensio**

MYAPP Pearson contiene tutto il materiale audio presente in questo libro.

L'app è disponibile per iOS e Android su Apple Store e GooglePlay Store.

Puoi accedere ai contenuti usando il QR Code presente sulla pagina a fianco. Dopo il primo utilizzo potrai ritrovare i contenuti nella Cronologia, oppure salvarli nei Preferiti.

Tutti i diritti riservati
© 2019, Pearson Italia, Milano-Torino
978 88 8339 4881 A

Per i passi antologici, per le citazioni, per le riproduzioni grafiche, cartografiche e fotografiche appartenenti alla proprietà di terzi, inseriti in quest'opera, l'editore è a disposizione degli aventi diritto non potuti reperire nonché per eventuali non volute omissioni e/o errori di attribuzione nei riferimenti.

È vietata la riproduzione, anche parziale o ad uso interno didattico, con qualsiasi mezzo, non autorizzata.
Le fotocopie per uso personale del lettore possono essere effettuate nei limiti del 15% di ciascun volume dietro pagamento alla SIAE del compenso previsto dall'art. 68, commi 4 e 5, della legge 22 aprile 1941, n. 633.
Le riproduzioni effettuate per finalità di carattere professionale, economico o commerciale o comunque per uso diverso da quello personale possono essere effettuate a seguito di specifica autorizzazione rilasciata da CLEAredi, Corso di Porta Romana 108, 20122 Milano, e-mail autorizzazioni@clearedi.org e sito web www.clearedi.org

Stampato per conto della casa editrice presso
Reggiani Print s.r.l - Brezzo di Bedero (Va)

Ristampa								Anno			
1	2	3	4	5	6	7	8	21	22	23	24

Referenze iconografiche

(a-alto; b-basso; c-centro; d-destra; s-sinistra)

123RF: 34 Sergiy Tryapitsyn; 46 wavebreakmediamicro; **Alamy**: 32 Guillem Lopez; 38 Russell Kord; 50 incamerastock; 52 Science History Images; 64 Niels Poulsen; 104 Imageplotter; 106ad Kevin Foy; 106bs Martin Thomas Photography; **Getty Images**: 101 SEBASTIEN FEVAL/AFP; 102 Photo12; **Shutterstock**: 30 Luboslav Tiles; 40 Steffen Foerster; 42 Iakov Filimonov; 44 Milosz Maslanka; 66 Standret.

Indice

INVALSI TRAINER

Listening Comprehension

Listening Comprehension 1	6
Listening Comprehension 2	7
Listening Comprehension 3	8
Listening Comprehension 4	9
Listening Comprehension 5	10
Listening Comprehension 6	11
Listening Comprehension 7	12
Listening Comprehension 8	13
Listening Comprehension 9	14
Listening Comprehension 10	15
Listening Comprehension 11	16
Listening Comprehension 12	17
Listening Comprehension 13	18
Listening Comprehension 14	19
Listening Comprehension 15	20
Listening Comprehension 16	21
Listening Comprehension 17	22
Listening Comprehension 18	23
Listening Comprehension 19	24
Listening Comprehension 20	25
Listening Comprehension 21	26
Listening Comprehension 22	27
Listening Comprehension 23	28
Listening Comprehension 24	29

Reading Comprehension

Reading Comprehension 1	30
Reading Comprehension 2	32
Reading Comprehension 3	34
Reading Comprehension 4	36
Reading Comprehension 5	38
Reading Comprehension 6	40
Reading Comprehension 7	42
Reading Comprehension 8	44
Reading Comprehension 9	46
Reading Comprehension 10	48
Reading Comprehension 11	50
Reading Comprehension 12	52
Reading Comprehension 13	54
Reading Comprehension 14	56
Reading Comprehension 15	58
Reading Comprehension 16	60
Reading Comprehension 17	62
Reading Comprehension 18	64
Reading Comprehension 19	66
Reading Comprehension 20	68
Reading Comprehension 21	70
Reading Comprehension 22	72
Reading Comprehension 23	74
Reading Comprehension 24	76
Reading Comprehension 25	78

Language Practice

Language Practice 1	80
Language Practice 2	81
Language Practice 3	82
Language Practice 4	83
Language Practice 5	84
Language Practice 6	85
Language Practice 7	86
Language Practice 8	87
Language Practice 9	88
Language Practice 10	89
Language Practice 11	90
Language Practice 12	91
Language Practice 13	92
Language Practice 14	93
Language Practice 15	94

SIMULAZIONE DI PROVA NAZIONALE

Listening Comprehension 1	96
Listening Comprehension 2	97
Listening Comprehension 3	98
Listening Comprehension 4	99
Listening Comprehension 5	100
Reading Comprehension 1	101
Reading Comprehension 2	104
Reading Comprehension 3	106
Reading Comprehension 4	108
Reading Comprehension 5	110
Griglie di valutazione	112

Cara Studentessa, caro Studente,

dall'anno scolastico 2018/2019 sono state introdotte all'ultimo anno della Scuola Secondaria di Secondo Grado le Prove Nazionali INVALSI per la lingua inglese.

Le prove vengono somministrate nella seconda parte dell'anno scolastico e costituiscono un requisito per l'ammissione all'Esame di Stato.

La prova viene svolta a computer ed è formata da due parti: nella prima parte viene testata la tua capacità di ascoltare e comprendere testi orali e nella seconda la tua capacità di leggere e comprendere testi scritti. Ci sono diverse tipologie di testo e la prova comprende diverse tipologie di task. Per ogni task avrai a disposizione delle istruzioni in inglese e un esempio che ti sarà utile per prendere familiarità con le domande della prova. Il numero di domande varia a seconda della prova.

Training for Successful INVALSI vuole fornire tutte le risorse necessarie per aiutarti ad affrontare la prova con gradualità e serenità. Troverai due sezioni:
- la prima parte, *INVALSI Trainer*, è stata pensata come una "palestra" in cui potrai esercitarti provando anche più volte a fare la prova o parte di essa, magari riflettendo sulle migliori strategie da usare o seguendo alcuni semplici consigli (*Tips and Strategies*). In questa prima parte, troverai 24 prove di ascolto e 25 prove di lettura, strutturate nelle diverse tipologie di task previste dalla prova e organizzate nei livelli B1 e B2 del Quadro Comune Europeo di Riferimento per le Lingue. Inoltre grazie alle attività di *Language Practice* potrai ripassare elementi lessicali o grammaticali, ma anche testuali e di uso della lingua che ti saranno utili per meglio comprendere e affrontare il test finale.
- La seconda parte ti propone una simulazione completa del test ufficiale. Una volta svolto il test potrai, verificando i punteggi ottenuti, sapere a che livello ti poni rispetto al task stesso.

Potrai svolgere tutti i task a casa oppure in classe scegliendo se farli "con carta e penna" oppure in modalità *computer based* su uno smartphone, un computer o un tablet grazie al Libro liquido, la versione online attivabile con il codice che trovi sulla copertina del libro.

Le tracce per le prove di *Listening Comprehension* possono essere ascoltate dal Libro liquido oppure scaricate attivando MYAPP Pearson mediante il codice QR che si trova nella pagina dell'indice.

Training for Successful INVALSI è stato pensato per allenarti ad affrontare al meglio la prova nazionale, ma anche per progredire nell'apprendimento della lingua inglese.

INVALSI TRAINER

In questa sezione troverai una serie di task di ascolto, di lettura e di uso della lingua che ti consentiranno di esercitarti in modo graduale alla prova che dovrai sostenere verso la fine del quinto anno della Scuola Secondaria di Secondo Grado.

I task sono organizzati secondo i livelli B1 e B2 del Quadro Comune Europeo di Riferimento per le Lingue e sono stati predisposti rispettando le tipologie previste e le caratteristiche indicate per la prova INVALSI.

Troverai attività di:
- *Multiple Choice Questions* (MCQ): domande a scelta multipla con quattro diverse opzioni di scelta;
- *Short Answer Questions* (SAQ): domande o frasi da completare con un massimo di quattro parole;
- *Multiple Matching* (MM): esercizi di abbinamento di diverse tipologie.

Per le varie tipologie di task troverai anche alcune indicazioni pratiche di lavoro che servono a mettere a fuoco le caratteristiche proprie di quel task, richiamando anche l'attenzione sulle opportune strategie da attivare.

Buon allenamento!

▶ INVALSI Trainer

Listening Comprehension 1
TASK Short Answer Questions

TIPS AND STRATEGIES
- Do not write more than the number of words the question asks for.
- Some questions will be concerned with the details. Questions about details will always contain keywords – words that focus on specific information or the most important ideas. Before the listening test starts, you should identify and underline these keywords to help you predict what to listen for.

🎧 **02** Listen to a text about a Michelin-starred restaurant in Singapore.

First you will have 1 minute to study the task below, then you will hear the recording twice. While listening, complete the sentences (1-8) using a maximum of 4 words.
The first one (0) has been done for you.

After the second listening, you will have 1 minute to check your answers.

0 The new Michelin-starred restaurant is situated in .... *Chinatown, Singapore* ....
1 The name of the restaurant is ....
2 The owner comes from ....
3 He learned how to cook from a chef ....
4 The total number of working hours per day is ....
5 The number of chickens he cooks in a day is now ....
6 The restaurant's special dish is Cantonese-style ....
7 The price for this speciality is approximately (give ONE answer)
   ....
8 The newly opened restaurant can seat up to ....

6

Listening Comprehension 2
TASK Short Answer Questions

INVALSI Trainer

TIPS AND STRATEGIES

- Look carefully at the question word being used, for example: *what*, *when*, *how many* … This should tell you what kind of information you need to listen for.
- Here are some common question words and the type of information they are most likely looking for.

Who	A name, a person, a company, a group or community, an institution, a job title.
When	A date, a time, a part of the day (*morning*, *evening*, etc.).
Where	A place.
Why	A reason, an explanation.
What	A specific thing, a name, an idea/opinion, one out of an unlimited choice.
Which	One out of a given or limited choice.
How	A description, way, manner, form or degree (e.g.: *how big*, *how well*, *how difficult*, etc.).
How often	Frequency (*monthly*, *daily*, *every hour*, etc.).
How much/many	Quantity, a number.

🎧 **03** Listen to the audio tour of the Main Library.

First you will have 1 minute to study the task below, then you will hear the recording twice. While listening, answer the questions (1-8) using a maximum of 4 words.
The first one (0) has been done for you.

After the second listening, you will have 1 minute to check your answers.

0	Who is in charge of the tour?	*A librarian.*
1	Where is the Lobby?	
2	How many areas does the Main Library have?	
3	How many storeys does the East Wing have?	
4	Where is the 'Quiet Study' area located?	
5	Where can you find the 'Reference Collection'?	
6	In which wing is the group study area?	
7	Where was one of the first wireless spots installed?	
8	What time does the Main Library usually close during the week?	

7

▶ *INVALSI Trainer*

Listening Comprehension 3
TASK Multiple Matching (Matching sentences)

B1

TIPS AND STRATEGIES
- Before listening, carefully read the numbered and lettered lists.
- The numbered list is usually in the same order as you will hear it in the recording.

🎧 04 Listen to Ms Roberts talking about cats and Girl, her own cat.

**First you will have 1 minute to study the task below, then you will hear the recording twice. While listening, match the beginnings of the sentences (1-7) with the sentence endings (A-J). There are two sentence endings that you do not need to use.
The first one (0) has been done for you.**

After the second listening, you will have 1 minute to check your answers.

[F] 0 Ms Roberts has had …
[ ] 1 Keeping a cat can be …
[ ] 2 She thinks the cat is …
[ ] 3 Ms Roberts would like to know …
[ ] 4 At present she has …
[ ] 5 Ms Roberts still remembers how Girl …
[ ] 6 Every day Ms Roberts and Girl …
[ ] 7 Ms Roberts has come to the conclusion Girl is …

A a funny animal.
B arrived in her life three years ago.
C what cats think of all day.
D spend time together.
E a lucky cat.
F lots of cats.
G something you can't avoid.
H how her cat sees her.
I a difficult decision to explain.
J only one cat.

Listening Comprehension 4
TASK Multiple Matching (Matching sentences)

INVALSI Trainer

B1

> **TIPS AND STRATEGIES**
> - In this type of question, you should listen for ideas, not for particular words or phrases.
> - The ideas in the lists might not be expressed in the same way as they are in the recording, so listen for synonyms and paraphrases.

🎧 05 Listen to two students, Chris and Mary, talking about school uniforms.

**First you will have 1 minute to study the task below, then you will hear the recording twice. While listening, match the beginnings of the sentences (1-7) with the sentence endings (A-J). There are two sentence endings that you do not need to use.
The first one (0) has been done for you.**

After the second listening, you will have 1 minute to check your answers.

- [F] 0 Mary doesn't like …
- [ ] 1 Chris thinks that wearing a uniform is …
- [ ] 2 Mary says uniforms reflect …
- [ ] 3 According to Mary, uniforms are …
- [ ] 4 Chris adds that school uniforms …
- [ ] 5 In Chris's view, organizing your apparel is ….
- [ ] 6 Mary wants …
- [ ] 7 Chris says uniforms are useful to …

A pointless traditions.
B a bit like organizing your mind.
C to wear a modern kind of uniform.
D diversity to be respected.
E help people focus on personality to get to know each other.
F having to conform to other people's preferences.
G something you can't avoid.
H an old idea of education.
I a way to be organized.
J promote a sense of belonging.

▶ *INVALSI Trainer*

Listening Comprehension 5
TASK Multiple Matching (Matching interview)

TIPS AND STRATEGIES
- Read all questions carefully.
- Use the information given to predict the types of answers you should be listening for.
- Listen carefully and match the options as you go.

🎧 06 Listen to Kathy Bell, a professional dancer, answering questions about her job and her diet.

First you will have 1 minute to study the task below, then you will hear the recording twice. While listening, match the interviewer's questions (A-I) with the answers (1-7). There is one extra question that you do not need to use.
The first one (0) has been done for you.

After the second listening, you will have 1 minute to check your answers.

- ☐ A What do you have for lunch?
- ☐ B Do you usually eat before a show?
- ☐ C What time does your dancing day usually finish?
- ☐ D Which means you eat like us mere mortals?
- [0] E What time do you get up in the morning? Do you have breakfast?
- ☐ F Can you tell us something about the schedule of a professional dancer?
- ☐ G How long does your morning class last?
- ☐ H What does a ballet dancer reach for when she's feeling hungry?
- ☐ I What about dinner?

INVALSI Trainer

Listening Comprehension 6
TASK Multiple Matching (Matching interview)

TIPS AND STRATEGIES
Focus on understanding what is being said, i.e. try to understand the whole conversation properly and only then mark your answer.

🎧 07 Listen to a writer answering questions about his travel habits.

First you will have 1 minute to study the task below, then you will hear the recording twice. While listening, match the interviewer's questions (A-K) with the answers (1-8). There are two extra questions that you do not need to use.
The first one (0) has been done for you.

After the second listening, you will have 1 minute to check your answers.

- ☐ A How many days a year do you spend on planes?
- ☐ B Where did you last go on holiday?
- ☐ C Who'd be someone you'd like to sit next to on a plane?
- ☐ D What do you always take along?
- 0 E Do you have a favourite destination?
- ☐ F Which do you prefer, long or short-haul flights?
- ☐ G As to hotels, what makes a good hotel good?
- ☐ H Got any travel-related advice for us?
- ☐ I Where do you never want to go again?
- ☐ J Do you bring your own camera with you?
- ☐ K What destination is an absolute must?

11

▶ *INVALSI Trainer*

Listening Comprehension 7
TASK Multiple Matching (Matching short texts)

> **TIPS AND STRATEGIES**
> It is impossible to guess the answer before you have heard the audio clip. In this kind of task, logical speculation or guesses won't work, so don't make any assumptions before you listen.

🎧 08 Listen to six alternative places for your free time in NYC.

**First you will have 1 minute to study the task below, then you will hear the recording twice. While listening, match the different places (1-6) with the headlines (A-I). There are two extra headlines that you do not need to use.
The first one (0) has been done for you.**

After the second listening, you will have 1 minute to check your answers.

- [F] 0 'My Fair Lady'
- [ ] 1 Jazz Age Night
- [ ] 2 Bamonte's
- [ ] 3 A champagne brunch sail
- [ ] 4 Grey Lady
- [ ] 5 The Lower East Side Tenement Museum
- [ ] 6 Bar Belly

A Bubbles abound
B Voices from the past
C Have a traditional Italian dinner
D Dance your way through the 20th century!
E Enjoy a late-night comedy
F More than fair!
G Ready to travel across space and time?
H The best retro party in modern New York
I Enjoy a summer cocktail

INVALSI Trainer

Listening Comprehension 8
TASK Multiple Choice Questions

 B1

TIPS AND STRATEGIES
- Before you listen, read through the questions carefully and circle the keywords to help you predict what to listen for.
- Read through the options. Some of them will be quite similar; highlight the words that distinguish them from each other. Three of the four options will contain some detail that makes them wrong.
- While reading through the options, try to think of synonyms or other ways to express these ideas; you might not hear the exact words in the recording, since the correct option may paraphrase what the speaker says.

🎧 09 Listen to a person talking about Key West.

First you will have 1 minute to study the task below, then you will hear the recording twice. While listening, choose the correct answer (A, B, C or D) for questions 1-8. Only one answer is correct. The first one (0) has been done for you.

After the second listening, you will have 1 minute to check your answers.

0 The speaker informs people about ...
- ☐ A places to visit on the island.
- ☐ B how to book a sightseeing tour.
- ☐ C when it's better to visit the island.
- ☒ D the modes of transportation available.

1 You should start your tour from the Old Town because it's ...
- ☐ A the centre of the island.
- ☐ B full of places to visit.
- ☐ C quite small.
- ☐ D a large pedestrian area.

2 You can go to Key West ...
- ☐ A by plane.
- ☐ B by taxi.
- ☐ C by ferry.
- ☐ D on foot.

3 Electric cars ...
- ☐ A can carry up to 4 people.
- ☐ B are very cheap to rent.
- ☐ C are perfect for long tours.
- ☐ D should be booked well in advance.

4 Scooters ...
- ☐ A are very expensive.
- ☐ B can be rented even for only one hour.
- ☐ C are the best mobility option of all.
- ☐ D are quite rare on the island.

5 A good idea for a sightseeing tour is ...
- ☐ A by private bus.
- ☐ B with an authorized local guide.
- ☐ C on a trolley.
- ☐ D in a car with a private driver.

6 Going around on foot ...
- ☐ A is seldom a good idea for solo travellers.
- ☐ B can be tiring and annoying.
- ☐ C is ideal if it's not hot or rainy.
- ☐ D lets you enjoy places from the inside.

7 The Historic Walking Tour and the Ghost Tour ...
- ☐ A take you around the Old Town.
- ☐ B are organized every day.
- ☐ C are the two most popular tours.
- ☐ D include audio-guides.

8 Take a boat to ...
- ☐ A go out to watch dolphins leaping from the water.
- ☐ B go sailing, windsurfing and snorkeling.
- ☐ C deepen your knowledge of marine wildlife.
- ☐ D the open sea in pursuit of the big catch.

▶ *INVALSI Trainer*

Listening Comprehension 9
TASK Multiple Choice Questions

TIPS AND STRATEGIES
- Read the question and come up with the answer in your head before looking at the options. Then choose the option that best matches the answer you came up with.
- Read all the options before choosing your answer, because some options may be only slightly different.
- Don't keep changing your answer; your first choice is usually the right one, unless you misread the question.

🎧 10 Listen to a radio news programme.

First you will have 1 minute to study the task below, then you will hear the recording twice.
While listening, choose the correct answer (A, B, C or D) for questions 1-8. Only one answer is correct.
The first one (0) has been done for you.

After the second listening, you will have 1 minute to check your answers.

0 Who is in hospital right now?
- ☐ A One of the robbers.
- ☐ B A policeman who has been wounded.
- ☒ C A man who tried to defend his shop.
- ☐ D A woman who tried to defend her store.

1 Who is George?
- ☐ A A policeman.
- ☐ B One of the robbers.
- ☐ C A reporter.
- ☐ D A shop owner.

2 When do the repairs to the local swimming pool start?
- ☐ A On Monday.
- ☐ B On Tuesday.
- ☐ C On Thursday.
- ☐ D The information is not given.

3 How long has the swimming pool been closed?
- ☐ A For six months.
- ☐ B Since last year.
- ☐ C Since yesterday.
- ☐ D Since June.

4 Why does the swimming pool need repairing?
- ☐ A Because it's been closed for a long time.
- ☐ B Because the swimming courses have been cancelled.
- ☐ C Because it's an old building.
- ☐ D Because of the damage caused by a storm.

5 How many students from the local School District will take part in the Scotland Yard Teen Academy?
- ☐ A Ten.
- ☐ B Seven.
- ☐ C Five.
- ☐ D Three.

6 How were the students selected?
- ☐ A With an interview.
- ☐ B Through a sports competition.
- ☐ C On the basis of their school results.
- ☐ D On the basis of an essay.

7 What's the weather like tomorrow?
- ☐ A Changeable all day.
- ☐ B Wet most of the day.
- ☐ C Strong winds and cold temperatures.
- ☐ D Mainly cloudy especially in the morning.

8 What kind of programme is this?
- ☐ A The weather forecast.
- ☐ B A local radio news programme.
- ☐ C Local news on a YouTube channel.
- ☐ D A live streaming programme on Twitter.

INVALSI Trainer

Listening Comprehension 10
TASK Short Answer Questions

B2

TIPS AND STRATEGIES
- Look through the sentences before you start to get an idea of what you will be hearing.
- Try to guess what type of information you need – is it a place, a name, a number, or something else?
- Remember that the words you see in the sentences may paraphrase the words from the audio, so listen out for words with similar meanings.
- Write the exact words, phrases or numbers that you hear to complete the sentences.
- If the answer is a number, you can write it using numerals (*200*) or you can write it out in words (*two hundred*).

🎧 **11** Listen to a text about a survey on cycling habits.

First you will have 1 minute to study the task below, then you will hear the recording twice.
While listening, complete the sentences (1-7) using a maximum of 4 words.
The first one (0) has been done for you.

After the second listening, you will have 1 minute to check your answers.

0	Reasons for riding a bike	*Health and fun / Enjoyment*
1	Total number of people who participated in the survey	
2	Total number of survey packs distributed	
3	% of people riding to work	
4	Total length of most journeys	
5	% of people who have had an accident	
6	% of respondents who only use a bike	
7	The survey was commissioned by	

▶ *INVALSI Trainer*

Listening Comprehension 11
TASK Short Answer Questions

TIPS AND STRATEGIES
- Read through the sentences, predict what types of answers you need for each gap and then listen to complete the sentences.
- Don't exceed the word limit.

🎧 **12** Listen to a chef talking about her daily routine.

First you will have 1 minute to study the task below, then you will hear the recording twice. While listening, complete the sentences (1-8) using a maximum of 4 words.
The first one (0) has been done for you.

After the second listening, you will have 1 minute to check your answers

0   Being a chef means *more than just cooking* .
1   The first task to complete in the morning is ....
2   The chef usually arrives earlier ....
3   Soups and desserts are usually prepared ....
4   People start arriving for lunch at ....
5   The chef and the staff have lunch ....
6   Beverages are usually delivered ....
7   The most hectic time of the day is ....
8   The next day's menu is planned ....

16

INVALSI Trainer

Listening Comprehension 12
TASK Short Answer Questions

TIPS AND STRATEGIES
- While listening, look for details and specific information, such as dates, places, numbers, opening hours, names ... If you hear them, but don't know where to place them yet, write them down in the margins.
- Later you will have some time to check your answers. If there are questions that you couldn't answer while listening to the passage, you might find that the notes you've made can help.

🎧 **13** Listen to a woman talking about the ideal places to visit in New York when travelling with children.

First you will have 1 minute to study the task below, then you will hear the recording twice.
While listening, answer the questions (1-8) using a maximum of 4 words.
The first one (0) has been done for you.

After the second listening, you will have 1 minute to check your answers.

0	When did she first go to New York?	*On her honeymoon.*
1	How long ago did she go to New York?	
2	What is the best way to visit New York?	
3	Where's the Alice in Wonderland statue?	
4	What kind of tour is the 'A Night at the Museum' tour?	
5	What is the High Line?	
6	Which of the places described is for pedestrians only?	
7	How long is the Brooklyn Bridge?	
8	What makes a walk on the Brooklyn Bridge dangerous?	

▶ *INVALSI Trainer*

Listening Comprehension 13
TASK Short Answer Questions

B2

TIPS AND STRATEGIES
- Pay careful attention to the grammatical structure of the sentence.
- You may have to change the speaker's words slightly in order to make them fit in the sentence correctly.

🎧 14 Listen to a text about Trieste.

First you will have 1 minute to study the task below, then you will hear the recording twice. While listening, complete the sentences (1-8) using a maximum of 4 words.
The first one (0) has been done for you.

After the second listening, you will have 1 minute to check your answers

0   The city used to base its own wealth on .... *trade* ....
1   Trieste's nickname was once ....
2   Today, Trieste's port is mainly used by ....
3   The Austrian royals once used Castle Miramare as ....
4   The Barcolana takes place every year on the ....
5   Trieste's Venetian castle dates back to ....
6   Trieste belonged to the Austro-Hungarian Empire from ....
7   Two Italian writers who lived and worked there were ....
8   The shape of Piazza Unità d'Italia is ....

18

Listening Comprehension 14

TASK Short Answer Questions

INVALSI Trainer

B2

> **TIPS AND STRATEGIES**
> If you miss a question, don't dwell on it because you may miss the answer to the next one.
> So, if you miss one, move on.

🎧 15 Listen to a text about Emilia Romagna.

First you will have 1 minute to study the task below, then you will hear the recording twice.
While listening, answer the questions (1-7) using a maximum of 4 words.
The first one (0) has been done for you.

After the second listening, you will have 1 minute to check your answers

0	What is Bologna's typical architecture style like?	*Medieval.*
1	How long is the present arcade system in Bologna?	....
2	What's Bologna's nickname?	....
3	Owing to its gastronomic tradition, how is Emilia Romagna also known?	....
4	How many natural regional parks are there in Emilia Romagna?	....
5	How tall is the highest peak in the Apennines?	....
6	How long is Italy's longest cycling path?	....
7	Among the many small villages, what is Dozza famous for?	....

19

▶ *INVALSI Trainer*

Listening Comprehension 15
TASK Multiple Matching (Matching sentences)

B2

TIPS AND STRATEGIES
- Speakers often use synonyms and paraphrases of keywords from the sentences you are trying to match, so be ready for this.
- Predicting how the options could be said differently to how they are written can help prepare you to catch the answer when it appears.

🎧 16 **Listen to Ben talking about why he loves burgers.**

First you will have 1 minute to study the task below, then you will hear the recording twice. While listening, match the beginnings of the sentences (1-7) with the sentence endings (A-J). There are two sentence endings that you do not need to use.
The first one (0) has been done for you.

After the second listening, you will have 1 minute to check your answers.

F	0	Ben prefers a burger to …
☐	1	His father used to …
☐	2	For his burgers Ben's father …
☐	3	They bought bread …
☐	4	Ben likes …
☐	5	A type of beef which is tender is …
☐	6	People in New York ask for …
☐	7	Burgers belong to …

A used only American cheese.
B thick medium-rare burgers.
C high quality burgers.
D Japanese Kobe.
E be a butcher.
F a steak.
G from an Italian bakery.
H every family's tradition.
I grill burgers at home.
J in a supermarket in Brooklyn.

20

INVALSI Trainer

Listening Comprehension 16
TASK Multiple Matching (Matching interview)

🎧 17 Listen to Nancy answering questions about her job: she's been working on how to make the Internet safer.

First you will have 1 minute to study the task below, then you will hear the recording twice. While listening, match the interviewer's questions (A-H) with the answers (1-5). There are two extra questions that you do not need to use.
The first one (0) has been done for you.

After the second listening, you will have 1 minute to check your answers.

☐ A What's the difference between online and real-life conversations?
☐ B Can you be more specific about that?
☐ C Are you also working on protecting elections from attack?
☐ D What online threats keep you up?
0 E What projects are you working on at the moment?
☐ F Are you a computer programmer or an analyst?
☐ G That sounds complicated... but is it feasible?
☐ H What's the ultimate objective of your work?

21

▶ *INVALSI Trainer*

Listening Comprehension 17
TASK Multiple Matching (Matching interview)

> **TIPS AND STRATEGIES**
> Don't immediately choose an answer if you hear exactly the same words because it may be a distractor. Distractors are wrong answers that seem right at first. For example, a speaker will say something and then he will correct himself or change his mind. So be careful when you think you hear the answer – it might be a distractor, you should keep listening to the end of that idea to be sure.

🎧 18 Listen to a person answering questions about climate change.

First you will have 1 minute to study the task below, then you will hear the recording twice. While listening, match the interviewer's questions (A-J) with the answers (1-7).
There are two extra questions that you do not need to use.
The first one (0) has been done for you.

After the second listening, you will have 1 minute to check your answers.

- ☐ A Who or what could help me understand and fight against climate change?
- ☐ B How did you start to get interested in climate change?
- ☐ C What's climate change?
- ☐ D Why do you think people don't believe that climate change is happening?
- [0] E Is it possible to stop climate change?
- ☐ F How is the climate likely to change in the future?
- ☐ G How has knowing about climate change influenced your life?
- ☐ H What do you think I should do to help save the earth?
- ☐ I Do we need a global government to address climate change?
- ☐ J What can we do to convince people that climate change is happening?

22

INVALSI Trainer

Listening Comprehension 18
TASK Multiple Matching (Matching speakers)

> **TIPS AND STRATEGIES**
> - Underlining keywords in the options is especially useful when you have long statements.
> - Be careful, because the speakers will not use exactly the same words as are in the options. When reading through the options, try to think of different ways to say the same thing since the correct option may paraphrase what the speaker says.

🎧 19 Listen to some people talking about their best travel memories.

**First you will have 1 minute to study the task below, then you will hear the recording twice. While listening, match the speakers (1-6) with their statements/headings (A-I). There are two extra statements/headings that you do not need to use.
The first one (0) has been done for you.**

After the second listening, you will have 1 minute to check your answers.

- ☐ A Driving along a unique road
- ☐ B Taking my sister to the UK
- ☐ C A very special train journey
- ☐ D Seeing all the lakes of Canada
- ☐ E Going on a river cruise
- [0] F In Germany to enjoy the spirit of Christmas
- ☐ G Back to my favourite island
- ☐ H Watching the sunset from a cabin in the woods
- ☐ I On a hiking tour in a national park

23

▶ *INVALSI Trainer*

Listening Comprehension 19
TASK Multiple Matching (Matching speakers)

TIPS AND STRATEGIES
- In this listening task, you will hear some short clips, each from a different speaker, on the same topic. There are ten options and you have to match the options to the speakers.
- There are some extra options that don't match any of the speakers.
- While listening, try to keep your eyes focused on all the options so that you can choose the right one.

🎧 **20** Listen to some people talking about social networking sites.

First you will have 1 minute to study the task below, then you will hear the recording twice. While listening, match the speakers (1-8) with their statements/headings (A-K). There are two extra statements/headings that you do not need to use.
The first one (0) has been done for you.

After the second listening, you will have 1 minute to check your answers.

☐ A Social media aids the spread of hate groups.
☐ B The use of social media can be correlated with personality and mental health disorders.
☐ C Being a part of a social media site can increase a person's quality of life.
☐ D Social media can induce people to waste time.
☐ E Students who are heavy social media users tend to have lower grades.
[0] F Social media sites help students socialize.
☐ G Social media posts can't be completely deleted.
☐ H Social media offers teachers platforms for collaboration with other teachers and communication with students outside the classroom.
☐ I Social media is good for the economy.
☐ J Social media facilitates political change.
☐ K Unauthorized sharing on social media exposes artists to loss of income.

Listening Comprehension 20
TASK Multiple Choice Questions

🎧 21 Listen to an interview with Mr Eugenijus Gefenas from Lithuania who is chairing UNESCO's Intergovernmental Bioethics Committee.

First you will have 1 minute to study the task below, then you will hear the recording twice. While listening, choose the correct answer (A, B, C or D) for questions 1-8. Only one answer is correct. The first one (0) has been done for you.

After the second listening, you will have 1 minute to check your answers.

0 How did Mr Gefenas discover his interest in bioethics?
   ☐ A His parents were both bioethicists.
   ☐ B He had to study bioethics at university.
   ☒ C He attended a lecture on bioethics.
   ☐ D After completing his studies in public health politics.

1 What is bioethics?
   ☐ A It is a branch of contemporary biology.
   ☐ B It is the study of what is really new in recent discoveries.
   ☐ C It is about discussing decisions concerning human life and health in everyday situations.
   ☐ D It is the study of the moral issue involved in complex situations having to do with human life and health.

2 How important in bioethics is the method you choose?
   ☐ A It's essential to follow the right method of inquiry.
   ☐ B It doesn't matter as much as the questions you ask.
   ☐ C Mr Gefenas doesn't mention the method of inquiry.
   ☐ D Bioethics doesn't have its own method.

3 Which situation is given as an example of a bioethics issue?
   ☐ A Lab experiments on animals.
   ☐ B End-of-life decisions.
   ☐ C Medical treatment for cancer.
   ☐ D The use of technologies.

4 What kind of scenario do we usually talk about in bioethics?
   ☐ A Perfect scenarios.
   ☐ B Bad scenarios.
   ☐ C Scenarios that are 'less bad' than others.
   ☐ D Only good scenarios.

5 How does Mr Gefenas describe the multidisciplinary factor?
   ☐ A In bioethics there are at least three people working together on the same problem.
   ☐ B When faced with a problem, a team of experts sharing the same view is called.
   ☐ C Problematic issues can be better dealt with by different disciplines.
   ☐ D Only a team of experts from different countries can lead to sound decisions.

6 What kinds of experts are usually called on?
   ☐ A Lawyers, engineers and doctors.
   ☐ B Doctors, philosophers and lawyers.
   ☐ C Biologists, engineers, and lawyers.
   ☐ D Teachers, doctors, and lawyers.

7 How long has UNESCO been involved in bioethics?
   ☐ A Since 1917.
   ☐ B Since the 1960s.
   ☐ C Since the 1970s.
   ☐ D For more than 70 years.

8 Why is it important for UNESCO to be involved in bioethics?
   ☐ A Because it's an international organization.
   ☐ B Because there are other organizations too.
   ☐ C Because it's a governmental organization.
   ☐ D Because it's a multidisciplinary organization.

▶ INVALSI Trainer

Listening Comprehension 21
TASK Multiple Choice Questions

TIPS AND STRATEGIES
When practising, don't just try to find the right answer. Also say why the wrong answers are wrong. That will help you build the skills you need to do well in the exam.

🎧 22 Listen to a person explaining how Johannesburg has been changing.

First you will have 1 minute to study the task below, then you will hear the recording twice. While listening, choose the correct answer (A, B, C or D) for questions 1-8. Only one answer is correct. The first one (0) has been done for you.

After the second listening, you will have 1 minute to check your answers.

0 Johannesburg …
- ☐ A owes its name to a miner.
- ☐ B is situated in a deserted area.
- ☒ C is the most important business town in South Africa.
- ☐ D is the capital of South Africa.

1 Johannesburg …
- ☐ A used to be a dangerous town in the '90s.
- ☐ B has a vast industrial area.
- ☐ C is surrounded by gold mines.
- ☐ D is, according to legend, a haunted town.

2 The city started to …
- ☐ A develop in the late '90s.
- ☐ B change its policy at the turn of the century.
- ☐ C attract people again after a terrible earthquake.
- ☐ D be a safe place to live again in 2008.

3 Efforts have been made to …
- ☐ A build a new train system.
- ☐ B turn the city centre into a cultural hub.
- ☐ C keep the demographic rise under control.
- ☐ D attract tourism and investments.

4 'Arts on Main' is …
- ☐ A the most important shopping centre of the town.
- ☐ B an old factory which has now become a museum.
- ☐ C a cultural centre full of activities.
- ☐ D the newest art gallery in town.

5 Soweto is …
- ☐ A an important tourist attraction.
- ☐ B a shanty town on the outskirts.
- ☐ C where the Apartheid Museum is.
- ☐ D full of modern buildings.

6 Lots of tourist attractions …
- ☐ A are available both in town and outside it.
- ☐ B still need investments.
- ☐ C cannot be reached by train.
- ☐ D tell the story of apartheid.

7 Pretoria …
- ☐ A can be visited on foot.
- ☐ B is full of green spaces.
- ☐ C has a famous lion park.
- ☐ D is not for tourists.

8 The Cradle of Humankind is …
- ☐ A now under restoration.
- ☐ B in Johannesburg's city centre.
- ☐ C home to some of the world's most ancient fossils.
- ☐ D visited every year by millions of people.

Listening Comprehension 22

TASK Multiple Choice Questions

B2

🎧 23 Listen to the news of a missing boy.

First you will have 1 minute to study the task below, then you will hear the recording twice. While listening, choose the correct answer (A, B, C or D) for questions 1-9. Only one answer is correct. The first one (0) has been done for you.

After the second listening, you will have 1 minute to check your answers.

0 Where did the boy go missing?
- ☐ A In Cambridge.
- ☐ B In Monkfield Park.
- ☒ C Near Cambridge.
- ☐ D In a nature reserve.

1 The police …
- ☐ A have already found the boy.
- ☐ B are still searching near the boy's school.
- ☐ C are searching far away from the boy's school.
- ☐ D have stopped looking for the boy.

2 The missing boy is …
- ☐ A Caribbean.
- ☐ B Caribbean/English.
- ☐ C English.
- ☐ D Indian/English.

3 He is …
- ☐ A taller than other 9-year-olds.
- ☐ B shorter than other 9-year-olds.
- ☐ C slimmer than other 9-year-olds.
- ☐ D as tall as other 9-year-olds.

4 His school uniform consists of: …
- ☐ A black trousers, a white polo shirt, a black sports jacket.
- ☐ B grey trousers and a white T-shirt.
- ☐ C grey trousers, a white polo shirt, a black sports jacket.
- ☐ D grey trousers, a white polo shirt, a black blazer.

5 What is the boy carrying with him?
- ☐ A A blue rucksack.
- ☐ B A black gym bag.
- ☐ C A black rucksack.
- ☐ D His school books.

6 Authorities think he left his school …
- ☐ A before 8:45.
- ☐ B at about 8:45 a.m.
- ☐ C at about 8:45 p.m.
- ☐ D at about 8:55.

7 The resident saw …
- ☐ A a lot of policemen.
- ☐ B the boy.
- ☐ C the boy's parents.
- ☐ D students in school uniforms.

8 Monkfield Park School principal …
- ☐ A announced a press conference.
- ☐ B didn't want to comment on the news.
- ☐ C commented on the news together with a County Council spokesperson.
- ☐ D commented on the news alone.

9 The police emergency number is …
- ☐ A 845.
- ☐ B 999.
- ☐ C 901.
- ☐ D 101.

▶ *INVALSI Trainer*

Listening Comprehension 23

TASK Multiple Choice Questions

TIPS AND STRATEGIES
- Don't just pick the first answer you hear. Make a small mark next to that choice and then continue listening to be sure that it is the correct one and the other options are wrong.
- Don't spend too much time on one question. If you don't get the answer or you are unsure, make an educated guess and move on.

🎧 **24** Listen to the presentation of 'Taking a walk near Argenteuil', a painting by Claude Monet.

First you will have 1 minute to study the task below, then you will hear the recording twice. While listening, choose the correct answer (A, B, C or D) for questions 1-8. Only one answer is correct. The first one (0) has been done for you.

After the second listening, you will have 1 minute to check your answers.

0 'Taking a walk near Argenteuil' was painted in …
- [X] A 1875.
- [ ] B 1785.
- [ ] C 1865.
- [ ] D 1758.

1 How many paintings did Monet make in Argenteuil?
- [ ] A 78.
- [ ] B 85.
- [ ] C 70.
- [ ] D 170.

2 What is the exact size of the painting?
- [ ] A 80 cm high and 60 cm wide.
- [ ] B 60 cm high and 18 cm wide.
- [ ] C 60 cm high and 80 cm wide.
- [ ] D 18 cm high and 60 cm wide.

3 How many people are in the painting?
- [ ] A A couple alone.
- [ ] B A couple with their children.
- [ ] C Three.
- [ ] D Two children and an adult.

4 What's the weather like?
- [ ] A It's a warm autumn day.
- [ ] B It's a hot summer day with a light breeze.
- [ ] C It's very windy and cloudy.
- [ ] D It's a rainy day.

5 What are the figures doing?
- [ ] A They are walking in a field full of flowers.
- [ ] B They are running among old trees.
- [ ] C They are having a picnic in a park.
- [ ] D They are relaxing under an old tree.

6 What is Camille wearing?
- [ ] A A white skirt and a white cap.
- [ ] B A white dress and a tall hat.
- [ ] C A colourful dress and a white hat.
- [ ] D A green blouse on a white skirt.

7 What is depicted in the foreground?
- [ ] A Flowers of different colours.
- [ ] B Some elderly figures.
- [ ] C Some old trees.
- [ ] D A field full of red poppies.

8 What kind of text is this?
- [ ] A An autobiography.
- [ ] B A description.
- [ ] C A public speech.
- [ ] D A lecture.

INVALSI Trainer

Listening Comprehension 24
TASK Multiple Choice Questions

B2

🎧 25 Listen to Andrea and Claire discussing their experiences abroad.

First you will have 1 minute to study the task below, then you will hear the recording twice. While listening, choose the correct answer (A, B, C or D) for questions 1-9. Only one answer is correct. The first one (0) has been done for you.

After the second listening, you will have 1 minute to check your answers.

0 The interview is with two young people who …
- [ ] A spent a year abroad.
- [ ] B went on holiday abroad.
- [X] C spent some time abroad studying.
- [ ] D haven't come back home yet.

1 Andrea and Claire …
- [ ] A both studied English abroad.
- [ ] B went to two different countries.
- [ ] C attended a photography course abroad.
- [ ] D don't think the experience is for everyone.

2 Andrea likes London because …
- [ ] A it offers lots of opportunities to young people.
- [ ] B it's a city full of modern buildings.
- [ ] C of its numerous sports facilities.
- [ ] D it's the perfect combination of things he knows and new things.

3 While in Greece Claire …
- [ ] A tried to mix with Greek people as much as possible.
- [ ] B also visited touristic places like Santorini.
- [ ] C adapted to all sorts of experiences.
- [ ] D didn't really like Greek weather.

4 According to Andrea, the most important cultural experience in London was …
- [ ] A shopping on Oxford Street.
- [ ] B going to a football match.
- [ ] C meeting people from other countries.
- [ ] D adapting to local food.

5 According to Claire, the most important cultural experience in Greece was …
- [ ] A visiting Mykonos and Santorini.
- [ ] B taking the Tube.
- [ ] C going to the sites.
- [ ] D studying the Classics.

6 What does Claire say about Greek food?
- [ ] A She didn't really like it.
- [ ] B She thinks it is too spicy.
- [ ] C She considers it a cultural experience.
- [ ] D She doesn't say anything about food.

7 What's the added value of an experience abroad?
- [ ] A You can learn a new language.
- [ ] B You can learn things you don't learn at school.
- [ ] C You meet people from other places.
- [ ] D You visit new, faraway places.

8 What's Claire's advice to a young person who wants to go abroad?
- [ ] A Keep in touch with your friends and family at home.
- [ ] B Try to meet new people in order not to get homesick.
- [ ] C Study the Classics.
- [ ] D Take advantage of all the opportunities you may encounter.

9 How do the students feel about their experience abroad?
- [ ] A Fully enthusiastic.
- [ ] B Sceptical but optimistic.
- [ ] C They don't think it's suitable for everyone.
- [ ] D They think every young person should try it.

29

▶ INVALSI Trainer

Reading Comprehension 1
TASK Short Answer Questions

B1

Read the offer about a holiday in a Tuscan villa, then answer the questions (1-7) using a maximum of 4 words.

The first one (0) has been done for you.

Holiday at a charming villa with a personal chef and private tour guides.
Visit Chianti, Florence, Pisa, Lucca, San Gimignano and more

Unpack your bags and enjoy a seven-night stay in a centuries-old villa in the splendid Tuscan countryside. Each morning you'll awake to aromas from the kitchen as the chef prepares the meals for the day. You'll visit markets and shops and discover the connection Italian culture has with its food. Enjoy reading a book in one of the many rooms throughout the villa or take a swim in the pool after your morning walk in the vineyards just outside the door. 5

Trip highlights

- Seven nights at a beautiful historic villa
- Italian cooking lessons
- Meals based on regional Italian menus
- Breakfast provided every day
- Personal tour guides for Florence, Siena and San Gimignano
- Ground transportation
- A relaxed schedule

The recipes include dishes from the south, the classic cuisine of the centre, and the delicate and refined dishes from the northern regions. All will lead you to understand how food is connected to the places it comes from. Whether it's a visit to the butcher or a tour of a local farm, you will experience in person the culinary culture of 10
the Italian people. All dishes prepared in the villa are authentic – distinctively and unmistakably Italian. You are welcome to observe and even get your hands messy learning how to make pasta, stuffed zucchini flowers or *biscotti*, which will adorn the table. 15

What really sets *Italian Culinary Tours* apart from other experiences and tours are the daily excursions lead by expert local guides. Join us on our visit to Siena, an all-day tour of the city of Florence and a stroll around San Gimignano, which is one of the most impressive medieval 20
hill towns in all of Italy. Other visits include Pisa, Lucca and other towns that provide great opportunities for sightseeing, shopping and dining.

TIPS AND STRATEGIES

Read the entire text and the questions before doing anything else: for this type of question, reading the questions first and then looking for answers in the passage is not a good way to start. You should first familiarize yourself with the passage so as to understand the context of the answers you are looking for. If you read the questions first, you may get confused and you will certainly lose time. So read the passage first, then answer the questions.

Identify the topic of the text: the topic is the general idea and can be summed up in a word or short phrase. On the INVALSI tests, there is a short description of the text you are going to read in the instructions. Make sure you read the description as it usually states the topic of the passage.
For example, in this task the topic is 'a holiday in a Tuscan villa'.
Questions or statements do not usually use the same words as in the text, but they keep the same meaning and may contain some keywords.

Answering strategy:
- Read the text first.
- Then read the questions and underline the keyword(s). Think about synonyms or paraphrases for these keywords.
- Use keywords to identify the paragraph or the part of the text which is likely to contain the answer.
- Read the paragraph you've found carefully and search for the answer.
- Once you've written the answer, check to make sure it doesn't exceed the word limit.

Tip: The order of questions can help you: the answer for question 4 will probably be between the answers for questions 3 and 5 in the text.

---

0 How long does the holiday last?
7 days / Seven days.

1 Where is the villa?

2 Who does the cooking?

3 What can you do in your free time at the villa?

4 Which meals are included in the package?

5 Where are the meals prepared?

6 How long is the tour of Florence?

7 Which town visits are included in the package?

▶ *INVALSI Trainer*

Reading Comprehension 2
TASK Short Answer Questions

> **TIPS AND STRATEGIES**
> - Try not to make assumptions that are not included in the passage. Just rely on the information given in the passage and only give answers that are mentioned in the passage. Do not rely on facts that are not in the text.
> - When reading the incomplete statements, think about what type of word (e.g. a noun, verb, adjective, etc.) can be used and try to predict the answer. Also, think about keywords and what synonyms or paraphrasing could replace them.

Read the text about the Edinburgh Festival Fringe, then complete the sentences (1-7) using a maximum of 4 words.

The first one (0) has been done for you.

Edinburgh Fringe by the numbers

While many large cities in Europe empty out in August, that's when Edinburgh fills up – with mimes, musicians, actors, artists, and the hundreds of thousands of people who come to watch them perform as part of the Edinburgh Festival Fringe.

5 This year, from August 3rd to 27th, the giant arts celebration will feature more than 3,000 free or ticketed shows at 300 spots around the city. It is an open access performing arts festival, meaning there is no selection committee, and anyone may participate, with any type of performance.

An adventurous spirit is key for attendees. You never know what you're going to get – but then again, that's more than half the fun.

10 **1947**: Fringe started as eight shows in five venues back in 1947. Last year's event played host to a total of 3,398 performers, who put on a total of 54,232 performances over three weeks.

2,696,884: tickets issued last year, a record-breaking number. Fringe attendance has grown at an average of 7.3% over the last three years.

520: pages in this year's festival programme, which includes descriptions
15 of each show, maps and venue information. Download it at edfringe.com.

1981: year the prestigious Edinburgh Comedy Award was first given. The inaugural prize – 1,500 pounds – was given to the then little-known quartet of Emma Thompson, Hugh Laurie, Stephen Fry and Tony Slattery.

62: countries with performers at last year's Fringe. Awareness of the festival is so widespread
20 that last year its website was visited by people from every nation across the globe with one exception: North Korea.

0	The Edinburgh Festival Fringe takes place every year during the month of .... *August* ....
1	This year's edition starts on ....
2	The total number of places where shows are usually performed is ....
3	The Fringe is for people with ....
4	The first Festival Fringe was organized in ....
5	The total number of shows performed in the first edition was ....
6	In its first edition, the Edinburgh Comedy Award was a prize which consisted of ....
7	The number of nations which took part in last year's edition was ....

▶ INVALSI Trainer

Reading Comprehension 3
TASK Short Answer Questions

> **TIPS AND STRATEGIES**
> There are five main kinds of reading comprehension questions. Once you're familiar with them, you will be able to notice important parts of the passage while reading, thus saving time.
>
> - **Main Idea questions:** ask for the central idea or significance of the passage.
> - **Specific Detail questions:** ask for explicitly stated ideas.
> - **Inference questions:** ask for a statement's intended meaning.
> - **Tone or Attitude questions:** test your ability to understand the opinion or emotional state of the author from the way he/she talks about the topic.
> - **Guessing Meaning from Context questions:** ask you to guess the meaning of a word by looking at the text around it.

Read the news about the missing teens found in Texas, then answer the questions (1-8) using a maximum of 4 words.

The first one (0) has been done for you.

Police: missing teens found in Texas

Three missing teens from Collin County were found in Frisco, Texas, Tuesday afternoon during a traffic stop with a 13-year-old girl behind the wheel. Frisco is about 30 miles away from the area where the teens disappeared early Tuesday morning.

'We're OK, thank you all', a woman, identified by Collin County Police as the mother
5 of 13-year-old Jennifer Stenton, told a reporter who wanted to ask her a few questions.

34

The police said Jennifer and her neighbour, 15-year-old Carol Bradford, took the car belonging to Jennifer's mother around 6:30 Tuesday morning. The two also took Carol's 10-year-old brother Tom with them.

'They could have met somebody or come across somebody who would have taken
10 advantage of the situation completely', said Sgt. Robert Nicholson from the Collin County Police Department.

Collin County Police were searching for the three teens until about 4:30 Tuesday afternoon when they drove past the Central Police Department. The car was stopped a few hundred yards from the Police Department and the police found 13-year-old Jennifer behind the
15 wheel.

"The first thing I asked her was 'Let me see your driver's license.' She said, 'I'm 14.' She's actually 13. It's kind of dangerous, a 13-year-old driving", said Chief Mark Williams from the local Police Department.

Collin County Police said the girls apparently came to Frisco to visit one of the girls' relatives,
20 but no one was at home. "Well, we think they were here in Frisco since early this morning", said Sgt. Nicholson. Frisco Police said local radio reports and social media played a big role in finding the three missing teens. "It was shared all over the county and there were local people here sharing it as well, so if they were here, they were going to be found. Definitely", said Chief Williams.
25 Collin County Police Department said it is unclear if any charges would be filed against the older girls. They also said this was a teachable moment for other parents to always be aware of their children's activities.

---

0 How old is Jennifer?
13 years old / 13 / Thirteen years old / Thirteen.

1 How old is Carol?

2 Whose car had the teens taken?

3 What time did they leave home?

4 How long did they disappear?

5 Who was driving when the police stopped the car?

6 Why did they go to Frisco?

7 Apart from people sharing on social media what else helped the Police?

8 What should parents always keep an eye on?

▶ INVALSI Trainer

Reading Comprehension 4

TASK Multiple Matching (Matching short texts)

Read the information about a literary tour in London, then choose the correct tour (A-E) to answer the questions (1-8). You can use a text more than once.

The first one (0) has been done for you.

LONDON
A Literary Tour

From Chaucer to Dickens, Shakespeare to Virginia Woolf, London has provided inspiration (and a home) to some of the English language's greatest writers. For a look at the city's literary history, read on. Here are a few spots for literature lovers touring London.

A The British Library

It's the country's biggest book repository with more than 150 million items in its collection, including manuscripts that date back 4,000 years. It is the second largest library in the world, behind the Library of Congress in the US. The Library's collection includes the Magna Carta, a Gutenberg Bible, Shakespeare's First Folio, and works from Jane Austen to the Beatles.

B 50 Gordon Square

A blue plaque marks the headquarters of the Bloomsbury Group, a group of writers, artists, and economists, who met here in the early 20th century, including Virginia Woolf, E.M. Forster, and John Maynard Keynes.

C The Charles Dickens Museum

A display of Dickensiana in the great author's only surviving London house. You can tour the museum at your own pace or sign up for one of the Costumed Tours on the third Saturday of every month, in which a housemaid wearing traditional clothes gives you a tour of the residence.

D Westminster Abbey

The list of famous people buried in Westminster Abbey is really long and Poets' Corner serves as a kind of literary hall of fame. Geoffrey Chaucer's tomb was placed here in 1556. That was the beginning of Poets' Corner, which has since served as a memorial to Britain's greatest cultural contributors. Charles Dickens, Thomas Hardy, Rudyard Kipling, and Alfred Tennyson are all interred here, and there are also several monuments commemorating famous writers whose remains are elsewhere, most notably Shakespeare, who is buried in Stratford-upon-Avon.

E Shakespeare's Globe Theatre

Finish your day of literary delights with dinner and a show at the recreated theatre of England's most famous playwright.

> **TIPS AND STRATEGIES**
> - If there are two or three options that are similar and could potentially match a paragraph, write their numbers beside the paragraph they might match and try to figure out the difference between the two questions. What are the keywords? How does this change the meaning? Which one matches the paragraph best?
> - If you still can't decide which one suits best, move on and come back to it later. The answer will normally be easier to find after you have matched some more questions.

Where should you go … ?

- [E] 0 to watch a play by Shakespeare
- [ ] 1 if the original version of the Magna Carta is your main interest
- [ ] 2 to visit a famous writer's residence
- [ ] 3 to have something to eat after a literary tour
- [ ] 4 to see the original versions of old manuscripts and books
- [ ] 5 to visit the tombs of some of the most famous writers
- [ ] 6 for the first published collection of Shakespeare's works
- [ ] 7 to see what is left of the place where intellectuals and artists met at the beginning of the last century
- [ ] 8 if you are in London on the third weekend of the month

▶ *INVALSI Trainer*

Reading Comprehension 5
TASK Multiple Matching (Gap-fill)

TIPS AND STRATEGIES
- Read the sentences that fill in the gaps and identify the topic of each sentence. Use this information to work out how they might logically fit into the sequence of the text.
- Read the sentences before and after each gap closely, and work out what function the missing sentence must have.
- Think about what the articles, pronouns, conjunctions and time expressions in the paragraphs or sentences might refer to. Use this information to understand how they might linguistically fit into the text.
- Make your decisions, not necessarily in order. Start with easier ones and save the harder ones for last.
- Finally, read through your completed text to make sure it makes sense.

Read the text about fireworks.
Parts of the text have been removed. Choose the correct part (A-K) for each gap (1-8). There are two extra parts that you do not need to use. Write your answers in the spaces provided.

The first one (0) has been done for you.

Fire in the sky

As Independence Day draws near, the nighttime sky will (0) ....C.... . Everywhere fireworks will explode in a dark sky to celebrate the Fourth of July.

Many people will take the Promethean power of (1) ...., lighting fireworks, sparklers and other such items in their own garden. However, we should never forget there may be
5 risks and dangers which should be taken into account when organizing a fireworks parade.

An important suggestion to make the Fourth of July safer than ever is to (2) .... and also remember that homemade fireworks can be deadly. Never attempt to make your own devices. Do not use kits that (3) .... Mixing fireworks chemicals can be dangerous work that (4) ....

10 Remember that fireworks are not toys. Do you know that fireworks that comply with the official safety regulations (5) .... a household match, and can cause burn injuries or ignite clothing if used improperly?

Here is some more advice to help you celebrate the Fourth of July safely:

- always read and follow label instructions
15 - have an adult present at all times
- buy from reliable fireworks retailers
- always ignite (6) ....
- keep water handy in case of an emergency
- never experiment or attempt to make your own fireworks
20 - light only one firework at a time
- never re-ignite (7) ....
- store fireworks in a cool, dry place
- never carry (8) ....
- never throw fireworks at another person
25 - do not shoot fireworks in metal or glass containers.

A	avoid fireworks that aren't clearly labeled with the name of the item
B	include a dazzling fireworks display
C	be filled with fireworks across the country
D	fireworks outdoors
E	dangerous illegal explosives like
F	fireworks into their own hands
G	is best left to the experts
H	fireworks in your pocket
I	are advertised for making homemade fireworks
J	burn at approximately the same temperature as
K	malfunctioning fireworks

▶ INVALSI Trainer

Reading Comprehension 6
TASK Multiple Matching (Gap-fill)

Read the text about what is happening to Foula Primary School.
Parts of the text have been removed. Choose the correct part (A-K) for each gap (1-8). There are two extra parts that you do not need to use. Write your answers in the spaces provided.

The first one (0) has been done for you.

Teacher sought for single-pupil school on Foula

Jayne Smith is (0) ...C... . The job is being advertised with a salary of £49,133 and (1) .... The closing date is Thursday and there has been interest from as far afield as South Africa and Azerbaijan.

Foula, about 20 miles west of the Shetland Mainland, (2) .... and has a population of just 32. It was the location for the 1937 Michael Powell film 'The Edge of the World'.

The school currently (3) .... Ms Smith, 38, told a local radio this morning: 'I have loved my time on Foula, it has just been amazing. Most of the time I have been there we (4) .... He has been in the upper stages of primary, so we have been able to go and visit Fair Isle, we have had lots of trips to the mainland, it has just been brilliant.'

Of her decision to leave in October, she said: 'When I came, I was initially going to do two years, (5) .... and then of course I got caught up with being there. But I feel it is (6) ....'

And of the type of person suited to the post, the departing teacher said: 'To be quite honest, (7) ...., it's got to be someone who's so adaptable and able to live in an isolated area. We can be cut off from the mainland for ... I think the longest time while I have been there has been three weeks that we (8) .... You have to be really resilient.'

The flight to the Shetland Mainland is 15 minutes, and the ferry journey is two-and-a-half hours.

INVALSI Trainer

> **TIPS AND STRATEGIES**
> - Read the sentences before and after each gap very closely. They are usually the most important sentences to help you guess what is missing.
> - There are usually some clues in the text. Look for them! The most common are:
>   – names and pronouns (*Ms Smith, she…*)
>   – chronology (*When I came …, and then …*)
>   – quotation marks (*'I have loved my time on Foula.'*)
>   – contrast words (*but*)
>   – verb tenses (*has been …, I got caught up …, I feel …*)
>   – cause and effect (*so …*)
>   – repetitions

A	is one of the UK's most remote inhabited islands
B	have had no ferry and no plane
C	leaving Foula Primary, in Shetland, after three-and-a-half years in the post
D	time to go and get back to the mainland
E	it's not an easy task
F	rented three-bedroom accommodation is available
G	have actually had just one pupil
H	the job is only a small part of it
I	I didn't intend to stay that long
J	I thought it would look good on my CV
K	has two pupils but one is leaving for high school in Lerwick at the end of the current term

▶ INVALSI Trainer

Reading Comprehension 7
TASK Multiple Matching (Gap-fill)

> **TIPS AND STRATEGIES**
> You don't have to fill in the answers in order – start with the one you think is the easiest and when you get to the most difficult one there will only be two answers left.

**Read the text about the historical roots of Women's Day.
Parts of the text have been removed. Choose the correct part (A-J) for each gap (1-7). There are two extra parts that you do not need to use. Write your answers in the spaces provided.**

The first one (0) has been done for you.

Mimosa flower and social change

The mimosa flower has become the symbolic gift to offer to women on Women's Day in more than 100 countries all over the world. (0) ....C....; it is actually a day of commemoration with a politically charged history.

In the early 1900s, oppressive unsafe work conditions and inequality in the workforce were
5 at their height, while Socialist Party movements for change such as (1) .... were getting more and more important. In those early years of the 20th century, International Women's Day (2) ...., but never on March 8. It wasn't until 1910, during an International Socialist meeting in Copenhagen, that an International Women's Day (3) .... The proposal was met with unanimous approval by representatives of more than 100 women from 17
10 countries on the grounds that it would be a day to celebrate the progress made by women over the years.

The movement for fair and safe labour practices gained momentum after the event known as the Triangle Shirtwaist factory fire on March 25, 1911 in which (4) ...., the majority of them women including many young immigrants from Europe. The Triangle Shirtwaist
15 fire represents the culmination of the women's rights movements around the world, and is (5) ....

42

In Italy the tradition of giving a mimosa flower on March 8 began during the WWII years. On March 8, 1945, Women's Day (6) ...., and the following year the mimosa appeared as a symbol of this day most likely because the mimosa blooms in early March.

20 In the Cold War climate of the 1950s the mimosa-gifting tradition was banned as (7) .... Attempts were made in Italian parliament to make the *Festa della Donna* a national day, but failed. In the 1970s the feminist movement in Italy brought about a rebirth of the mimosa as a symbol of women's solidarity.

- **A** was officially established
- **B** a useless waste of time
- **C** a holiday that today often implies light-hearted socializing with female friends
- **D** was celebrated to honour freedom in liberated Italy
- **E** movements for women's rights
- **F** campaigns for equality, suffrage and better working conditions
- **G** 146 employees of the company died
- **H** a public disturbance
- **I** was commemorated on various spring days
- **J** one of the specific events remembered on this day

▶ INVALSI Trainer

Reading Comprehension 8
TASK Multiple Matching (Gap-fill)

B1

> **TIPS AND STRATEGIES**
> - When you're practising this part of the INVALSI test, underline the part of the text that you think matches the question. Underlining your reasons will help you see why you made mistakes if you miss a question.
> - You should be prepared to change your first answers, because you may change your mind when you read the text more carefully.

Read the text about Wellington.
Parts of the text have been removed. Choose the correct part (A-J) for each gap (1-7). There are two extra parts that you do not need to use. Write your answers in the spaces provided.

The first one (0) has been done for you.

Why is Wellington the best city in the world?

Wellington has recently been named the world's coolest little capital. It has all you can ask for – beaches, views, culture, music, film and plenty of dining options.

Here are the reasons why Wellington should be on your 'must visit' list.

Good coffee everywhere

5 In Wellington, bad coffee doesn't exist. (0) __C__ .

Hipsters' paradise

If you aren't already a hipster, you (1) ...., after trying Welly's famous craft beer, craft soda, artisan bread, and artisan dumplings. You can even enjoy a freshly baked bagel at the airport, (2) .... Gandalf riding a giant eagle, suspended above your head.

44

10 **Apart from that …**

Beyond the city limits, day-trippers can take in a great variety of bush and beach scenes. Not to mention (3) .... , with a stop to refuel at one of Wellington's many excellent cafés.

Take a breath, count to ten

Wellington is one of the greenest, most unpolluted cities in the world. It's windy – that's
15 true. But the wind (4) ....

Get cultured

Wellington has a reputation as an important cultural centre. And all it has to offer is within a compact two kilometres of city streets. You could enjoy a visit to Te Papa, the country's national museum, or a boat trip (5) .... Why not spend a day at the wildlife
20 bird sanctuary Zealandia; or maybe you could geek out over the 'Lord of the Rings' paraphernalia at Peter Jackson's Weta Cave, then (6) .... You can indulge in shopping and gastronomic delights all within a short walk of downtown hotels.

No matter what you're into, you can find something to do in Wellington and you (7) .... So what are you waiting for? Pack your bags and come for a visit – you won't regret it.

A   accompanied by a cold pressed juice and
B   If you wanted to, you could fill every day of your week with something new
C   Wellingtonians are proud to serve awesome brews
D   grab dinner and a movie at The Roxy Cinema in Miramar
E   It has thus beaten out Edinburgh and Melbourne for the top spot
F   will be by the time you leave
G   will only help you enjoy the fresh, clean air of the city
H   'll love every second of it
I   a drive along the bays on a nice day
J   to Somes Island, a scientific nature reserve

▶ INVALSI Trainer

Reading Comprehension 9
TASK Multiple Choice Questions

> **TIPS AND STRATEGIES**
> - Distractors look like the correct answer at first glance but are actually incorrect. When you locate the relevant section in the reading text, there will appear to be two or three plausible answers, but only one of them is actually correct.
> - Because there are so many distractors, sometimes 'correct' answers will seem to jump out at you. Don't be hasty: if you don't read the text carefully, you are more likely to choose an incorrect answer. Take some time to really understand the meaning of each option and what distinguishes one from another.

Read the text giving tips on how to barbecue food, then choose the correct answer (A, B, C or D) for questions 1-8. Only one answer is correct.

The first one (0) has been done for you.

Barbecue tips

Cooking food over fire has been a favourite method of food preparation since the beginning of time. Nothing is more irresistible
5   than the flavour and smoky aroma of barbecue. With a few quick tips this old cooking method can be fast and easy for everyone.

Here are some time savers that can
10 speed up barbecuing and let you enjoy the pleasures of the grill even in busy periods.

- Put all you need on a tray before you start grilling. You won't have to run back to the kitchen for a forgotten ingredient or tool. Keep seasoning, sauces and a timer handy
15   at all times.

- Keep your charcoal dry. It will light faster.

- Food will cook faster in a covered grill because heat is more confined. Remember that every time you take the cover off the grill you lose heat, which takes time to build up again. Choose ingredients with similar cooking times that do not require frequent timing.

20 • Nothing beats kebabs for speed. Cut boneless meat, poultry or fish into pieces and put them in olive oil and lemon juice with herbs of your choice. Kebabs can be prepared hours ahead or even the night before. All you need to do on a busy weekday is prepare them by adding vegetables and then grill them. Five to ten minutes with frequent turning is usually enough.

25 • Use a microwave to save time. Microwaving chicken parts for three to five minutes will save about ten minutes on the grill without any loss of flavour. Use a microwave with larger cuts of meat for five minutes. This will allow you to save ten to fifteen minutes on the grill. It also makes fast work of pre-cooking spareribs to render fat. Or use a microwave to bring steaks up to room temperature for faster cooking and tender,
30   more succulent meat.

46

0   Barbecuing …
    ☐ A was invented a few centuries ago.
    ☐ B dates back to the 19th century.
    ☐ C was brought to Europe from colonies.
    ☒ D is an old method of cooking food.

1   This list of advice …
    ☐ A could help people save time with BBQ.
    ☐ B is for experts.
    ☐ C also refers to a collection of traditional recipes.
    ☐ D is for those who like grilling food in their free time.

2   Before you start barbecuing …
    ☐ A assemble all you need on a plate.
    ☐ B check tools and ingredients are ready for use on the kitchen table.
    ☐ C decide what sauces you want to use.
    ☐ D set a clock to keep time under control.

3   The charcoal you use should be …
    ☐ A already on the grill.
    ☐ B the same every time.
    ☐ C dry.
    ☐ D prepared the day before.

4   Keep the grill covered as much as you can to …
    ☐ A keep heat outside and warmth inside.
    ☐ B save cooking time.
    ☐ C protect the food from insects.
    ☐ D cook all the ingredients at the same time.

5   You should uncover the grill …
    ☐ A on no occasion.
    ☐ B to keep the right temperature inside.
    ☐ C if and when you really need to.
    ☐ D when it's about time to serve the food.

6   Kebabs are …
    ☐ A made only with vegetables.
    ☐ B very long to prepare but taste delicious.
    ☐ C for people who don't like fish.
    ☐ D cubes of meat or fish which are marinated before grilling.

7   Use a microwave for pre-cooking food …
    ☐ A only when needed.
    ☐ B in case of bad weather.
    ☐ C whenever you are in a hurry.
    ☐ D only with certain types of meat.

8   Ribs lose fat faster if …
    ☐ A pre-cooked.
    ☐ B put directly on the grill.
    ☐ C grilled at high temperatures.
    ☐ D you leave them on a plate after grilling.

▶ *INVALSI Trainer*

Reading Comprehension 10
TASK Multiple Choice Questions

TIPS AND STRATEGIES
If you really have no idea which is the correct answer, you should start by crossing out the ones that you are sure are wrong. Then make a reasonable guess from the ones that remain.

Read the text about the importance of digital skills, then choose the correct answer (A, B, C or D) for questions 1-7. Only one answer is correct.

The first one (0) has been done for you.

Digital skills: what are they? And why are they so important?

The social and economic impact of technology is widespread and accelerating. The speed and volume of information have increased exponentially. Experts are predicting that 90% of the entire population will be connected to the Internet within ten years. With the Internet of things, the digital and physical worlds will soon be merged. These changes
5   herald exciting possibilities. But they also create uncertainty. And our kids are at the centre of this dynamic change.

Children are using digital technologies and media at increasingly younger ages and for longer periods of time. They spend an average of seven hours a day in front of screens – from televisions and computers to mobile phones and various digital devices. This is
10   more than the time children spend with their parents or in school. As such, it can have a significant impact on their health and well-being. What digital content they consume, who they meet online and how much time they spend on screen – all these factors will greatly influence children's overall development.

In the digital world kids are also exposed to many risks, such as cyberbullying, technology
15   addiction, obscene and violent content, and data theft.

Moreover, there is the digital age gap. The way children use technology is very different from adults. This gap makes it difficult for parents and educators to fully understand the risks and threats that children could face online. As a result, adults may feel unable to advise children on the safe and responsible use of digital technologies. Likewise, this gap
20   gives rise to different perspectives of what is considered acceptable behaviour.

So how can we prepare our children for the digital age? Without a doubt, it is critical for us to equip them with digital intelligence. Digital intelligence or 'DQ' is the set of social, emotional and cognitive abilities that enable individuals to face the challenges and adapt to the demands of digital life.

25   These abilities can broadly be broken down into eight interconnected areas: digital identity, digital use, digital safety, digital security, digital emotional intelligence, digital communication, digital literacy, digital rights.

Above all, the acquisition of these abilities should be rooted in desirable human values such as respect, empathy and prudence. These values facilitate the wise and responsible use
30   of technology.

(adapted from https://www.weforum.org/agenda/
2016/06/8-digital-skills-we-must-teach-our-children)

INVALSI Trainer

0 The main technological change is in …
- [ ] A how we share new information.
- [ ] B how fast we manage to communicate.
- [ ] C the type of social media we use.
- [X] D the speed and quantity of information we have.

1 Within the next decade …
- [ ] A most of the world's population will be connected.
- [ ] B technological changes will lead to an economic boom.
- [ ] C we will all have multiple digital identities.
- [ ] D cyber threats will become even more problematic.

2 The interconnection of everyday objects via the net is …
- [ ] A the Internet of things.
- [ ] B the main impact of technology.
- [ ] C a system of digital devices.
- [ ] D new digital content.

3 What does 'dynamic' (line 6) mean?
- [ ] A Fluid.
- [ ] B Rapid.
- [ ] C Vigorous.
- [ ] D Complex.

4 How is the use of digital technologies changing among children?
- [ ] A They use digital and media technologies at school and not only at home.
- [ ] B They start using digital and media technologies at a younger age.
- [ ] C They are using digital technologies much less than in the past.
- [ ] D They are now more aware of the risks than they were in the past.

5 What is particularly affected by the way children use technologies?
- [ ] A Their school results.
- [ ] B The relationship with other people.
- [ ] C Their health.
- [ ] D Their free time activities.

6 How does the text explain the 'digital age gap'?
- [ ] A Children can rely on adults for advice on the use of technologies.
- [ ] B Adults can't do many of the things children do with modern technologies.
- [ ] C Children use technologies in a less responsible way.
- [ ] D Adults and children don't use digital technologies in the same way.

7 What is 'digital intelligence' (line 22)?
- [ ] A The ability to communicate and collaborate with others online.
- [ ] B The ability to find, evaluate, utilize, share and create content.
- [ ] C The ability to acquire and apply new knowledge and skills related to digital technologies.
- [ ] D The ability to create and manage one's online identity and reputation.

▶ INVALSI Trainer

Reading Comprehension 11

TASK Short Answer Questions

> **TIPS AND STRATEGIES**
> Answer easy questions first. When encountering questions you are not very sure about, move on to easier ones. Return to more challenging questions once you've answered all the questions for which you know the answer. In some cases, you can decipher clues to answers for difficult questions from the questions you've already answered.

Read the text about the passion for Scrabble that Professor Martin Hayward has, then answer the questions (1-7) using a maximum of 4 words.

The first one (0) has been done for you.

Word up

Professor of Mathematics Martin Hayward is truly a man of letters – especially the kind found on Scrabble boards. Professor Hayward has been playing the famous word game since high school, for fun and in recent years for competition, and next month will return to one of its signature events, the National Scrabble Championship, which will take place in Cardiff
5 from Sept. 4-8.

It will be the fifth time Hayward has been to the tournament, which is divided into four divisions: Elite, Expert, Intermediate and Novice. Professor Hayward will make his debut in the Intermediate category this go-round. Although relatively new to competitive Scrabble, he's played in some 40 tournaments over the past decade.

10 Every player plays 31 rounds at the tournament, which works out to eight games and roughly eight hours a day for the first four days. Three games make up the final part of competition. 'I enjoy the thrill of the game. I know there's prize money for finishing first but I don't mind. What is really important to me is to give the best performance I can,' he explains. 'I also really like being around others who share my love for Scrabble. It's a small,
15 tightly-knit community so over time you get to know quite a few people.'

50

Introduced to the game by 'a very smart colleague of mine', a linguist ('I only beat him once in ten games'), Hayward discovered through Scrabble an interest in language and a fascination with unusual words. And of course he also enjoys the mathematical and analytical aspects of the game, and the strategies which go with them: 'You have to
20 work out how playing a particular word will affect your opponent's moves and your own following moves.'

There's even a visual appeal to Scrabble, Hayward adds. 'As a game progresses you become aware of the beauty of the spatial patterns that appear on the game board.'

As someone who takes the game seriously enough to play it on a weekly basis, Professor
25 Hayward studies the Scrabble Dictionary for a half-hour every day. But it's not a random scanning of pages: "It helps to have a study programme. Some look for long words that may not actually appear. I look for 'high probability' words, with an emphasis on learning or reviewing seven- or eight-letter words, as well as 'fives' – there are about 9,000 of them."

Professor Hayward will have more time for Scrabble after his retirement, which is due
30 at the end of next academic year. He would like to continue his efforts to teach Scrabble to his grandchildren.

0	How long has Professor Martin Hayward been playing Scrabble?	
	Since high school.	
1	How long has he been playing Scrabble at a professional level?	
2	How long does the National Scrabble Championship last?	
3	How many times has he already taken part in the National Scrabble Championship?	
4	Which level does Professor Hayward currently belong to?	
5	How did Professor Hayward discover Scrabble?	
6	How often does he play Scrabble?	
7	How many five-letter words are there in the Scrabble Dictionary?	

 INVALSI Trainer

Reading Comprehension 12
TASK Short Answer Questions

 B2

TIPS AND STRATEGIES
- Read the instructions carefully and note the word limit.
- Take time to understand the question fully: this allows you to know exactly what to look for in the text.
- Underline the keywords in the questions.
- Read the text and find the part that probably contains the answer; read that part attentively, searching for the answer.
- Once you have the answer, make sure you don't exceed the word limit specified in the instructions.

Read the biography of Leonardo da Vinci, then answer the questions (1-7) using a maximum of 4 words.

The first one (0) has been done for you.

Leonardo da Vinci

Da Vinci was one of the great creative minds of the Italian Renaissance, hugely influential as an artist and sculptor but also immensely talented as an engineer, scientist and inventor.

Leonardo da Vinci was born on 15 April 1452 near the Tuscan town of Vinci, the illegitimate son of a local lawyer.
5   Little is known about Leonardo's early life. He spent his first five years in the village of Anchiano, then lived in the household of his father, grandparents and uncle, Francesco, in the small town of Vinci. Leonardo was taken to Florence by his father to begin his apprenticeship in the
10 studio of the sculptor and painter Andrea del Verrocchio in the 1470s when Verrocchio was working on the bronze bell for the Cathedral. Verrocchio's workshop was the most important in Florence and, besides Leonardo, it 'generated' artists such as Botticelli and Perugino. The
15 workshop produced marble and bronze statues, painted panels, and goldwork. It was here that Leonardo learned techniques that formed him as an artist and became an enthusiastic experimenter. In 'The Baptism of Christ', at the Uffizi Gallery in Florence, you can see the hand
20 of Leonardo at the age of 16 when he was part of Verrocchio's workshop.

By 1472, at the age of 20, Leonardo qualified as a master in the Guild of Saint Luke, the guild of artists and doctors of medicine. Leonardo's earliest known dated work is a drawing in pen and ink of the Arno valley, drawn on 5 August 1473.

25 In 1478 Leonardo became an independent master. In about 1483, he moved to Milan to work for the ruling Sforza family as an engineer, sculptor, painter and architect. From 1495 to 1497 he produced a mural of 'The Last Supper' in the refectory of the Monastery of Santa Maria delle Grazie, in Milan. His work for Ludovico il Moro, Duke of Milan, included pageants for special occasions, designs for a dome for the Milan Cathedral and a model for
30 a huge equestrian monument to Francesco Sforza, Ludovico's predecessor.

Leonardo modelled a huge horse in clay, which became known as the 'Gran Cavallo'. Seventy tons of bronze were set aside to cast it. The monument remained unfinished for

52

several years, which was not unusual for Leonardo. In 1492 the model was completed, and Leonardo was making detailed plans for its casting. Michelangelo rudely implied that
35 Leonardo was unable to cast it. In November 1494, Ludovico gave the bronze to be used for cannons to defend the city from invasion by Charles VIII. After Milan was invaded by the French, Leonardo left the town. He may have visited Venice before returning to Florence.

During his time in Florence, he painted several portraits, but the only one that survives is the famous 'Mona Lisa' (1503-1506).

40 It was in 1506 that Leonardo chose the Parco di Montececeri in Fiesole as the starting point for his experiment with his 'flying machine'. Now inside the park, in memory of the first-ever attempt to fly, stands a monument that carries Leonardo's epigraph. The monument is located in a small panoramic point where Leonardo's machine first took flight.

In 1507, da Vinci returned to Milan, remaining there until 1513. This was followed by three
45 years based in Rome. In 1517, at the invitation of the French king Francis I, Leonardo moved to the Château of Cloux, near Amboise in France, where he died on 2 May 1519.

0 What was Leonardo's father?
A lawyer / He was a lawyer.

1 Where did Leonardo live as a child?

2 When did Leonardo become an apprentice in Florence?

3 How old was Leonardo when he became a master?

4 What did he paint in Milan?

5 Where did Leonardo move to after the French occupied Milan?

6 What did Leonardo experiment with in Fiesole?

7 Where did Leonardo die?

▶ INVALSI Trainer

Reading Comprehension 13

B2

TASK Multiple Matching (Matching sentences)

Read the text about radioactivity in everyday life, match the beginnings of the sentences (1-8) with the sentence endings (A-K). There are two sentence endings that you do not need to use.

The first one (0) has been done for you.

Radioactivity in everyday life

Radioactivity is a part of our Earth. Naturally occurring radioactive materials are in the Earth's crust, the floors and walls of our homes, schools or offices, and in the food we eat and drink. There are radioactive gases in the air we breathe. Our own bodies contain naturally occurring radioactive elements.

5 Man has always been exposed to natural radiation arising from the Earth as well as from outside the Earth. The radiation we receive from outer space is called cosmic radiation or cosmic rays.
We also receive exposure from man-made radiation, such as X-rays, radiation used to diagnose diseases and for cancer therapy. Fallout from nuclear explosives testing, and small
10 quantities of radioactive materials released into the environment from coal and nuclear power plants, are also sources of radiation exposure to man.

Everything we encounter in our daily lives contains some radioactive material. Careful analysis can identify and quantify the radioactive material in just about anything. What follows is a description of a few of the most commonly encountered and familiar consumer
15 products that can contain sufficient radioactive material for it to be distinguished with a simple handheld radiation survey metre.

Watches and clocks

Modern watches and clocks sometimes use a small quantity of hydrogen-3 (tritium) or promethium-147 as a source of light. Older (for example, pre-1970) watches and clocks used
20 radium-226 as a source of light. If these older timepieces are opened and the dial or hands handled, some of the radium could be picked up and possibly ingested. As such, caution should be exercised when handling these items.

Ceramics

Ceramic materials (for example, tiles, pottery) often contain elevated levels of naturally
25 occurring uranium, thorium, and/or potassium. In many cases, the activity is concentrated in the glaze. Unless there is a large quantity of the material, readings above a background level are unlikely. Nevertheless, some older (for example, pre-1960) tiles and pottery, especially those with an orange-red glaze, can be quite radioactive.

Smoke detectors

30 Most of them contain a low-activity americium-241 source. Alpha particles emitted by the americium ionize the air, making the air conductive. Despite the fact that these devices save lives, the question 'are smoke detectors safe?' is still asked by those with an inordinate fear of radiation. The answer, of course, is 'yes, they are safe'. Instructions for proper installation, handling and disposal of smoke detectors are found on the package.

35 ### Glass

Glassware, especially antique glassware with a yellow or greenish colour, can contain easily detectable quantities of uranium. Even ordinary glass can contain high-enough levels of

54

potassium-40 or thorium-232 to be detectable with a survey instrument. Older camera lenses (1950s-1970s) often employed coatings of thorium-232 to alter the index of refraction.

40 **Food**

Food contains a variety of different types and amounts of naturally occurring radioactive materials. Although the relatively small quantities of food in the home contain too little radioactivity to be readily detectable, major shipments of food have been known to set off the alarms of radiation monitors at border crossings.

45 **Antique radioactive curative products**

In the past, primarily 1920 through 1950, a wide range of radioactive products were sold as cure-alls, for example, radium-containing pills, pads, solutions and devices designed to add radon to drinking water. Most such devices are relatively harmless, but occasionally one can be encountered that contains potentially hazardous levels of radium.

Information taken from a Health Physics Society fact sheet,
'Consumer Products Containing Radioactive Materials', published in November 2002.
(*adapted from* https://hps.org/publicinformation/ate/faqs/consumerproducts.html)

| F | 0 | Since the beginning of time all living creatures …
| ☐ | 1 | Examples of artificial sources of radiation include …
| ☐ | 2 | A handheld radiation survey meter is ….
| ☐ | 3 | As older watches can contain radioactive materials ….
| ☐ | 4 | In ceramics the most radioactive parts are …
| ☐ | 5 | The word 'background' (line 26) refers to …
| ☐ | 6 | Smoke detectors are safe …
| ☐ | 7 | Camera manufacturers used to design lenses …
| ☐ | 8 | Food may contain …

A small enough to hold in your hand when using it.
B usually found on the decorative surface coating.
C a type of radiation which is produced artificially.
D as long as we handle them properly.
E employing radioactive glass in one or more elements.
F have been exposed to radiation.
G too little radioactivity to be detected.
H they should be handled with special care.
I devices such as the equipment used in medical applications.
J different amounts of naturally occurring radioactive materials.
K the radiation found naturally on Earth.

▶ *INVALSI Trainer*

Reading Comprehension 14
TASK Multiple Matching (Matching sentences)

B2

Read the text about UNESCO's Man and the Biosphere Programme, then match the beginnings of the sentences (1-8) with the sentence endings (A-K). There are two sentence endings that you do not need to use.

The first one (0) has been done for you.

UNESCO's Man and the Biosphere Programme (MAB)

Launched in 1971, UNESCO's Man and the Biosphere Programme (MAB) aims to improve relationships between people and their environments. MAB tries to promote innovative approaches to economic development that are socially and culturally appropriate, and environmentally sustainable. The MAB Programme predicts the consequences of today's
5 actions on tomorrow's world and thereby increases people's ability to efficiently manage natural resources for the well-being of both human populations and the environment.

It has developed a World Network of Biosphere Reserves which currently counts 701 sites in 124 countries all over the world, including 21 transboundary sites. It is considered a dynamic and interactive network of sites of excellence. It works to foster the harmonious integration
10 of people and nature for sustainable development through participatory dialogue, knowledge sharing, poverty reduction, increased human well-being, respect for cultural values and by improving society's ability to cope with climate change.

Biosphere reserves harmonize the conservation of biological and cultural diversity with economic and social development, through partnerships between people and nature.
15 They also contribute to the transition to green societies by experimenting with green development options such as sustainable tourism.

Here are some success stories and good practices in different biosphere reserves around the world.

Russian Federation: the new power station in the Altaisky biosphere reserves is the only
20 one to use solar energy in the country. It supplies a large village with electricity 24 hours a day. Previously the village had used an old diesel generator and electricity was supplied only during the daytime.

Slovenia: within the Škocjan Caves Park School Network, 12- to 14-year-old secondary school students from Slovenia and Italy explore research topics related to the Reka River, one of the
25 largest sinking rivers in the world.

Brazil: the Serra do Espinhaço Biosphere Reserve happens to be the most intensely mined biosphere reserve in the world. The compensation that municipalities receive from mining companies remains their greatest source of income but an ecological tax introduced nearly 20 years ago is making conservation an attractive alternative investment option
30 for municipalities.

Jordan: the jobs created by the reserve since its establishment in 1985 mark the first time in generations that many local residents have been afforded viable economic opportunities that are also sustainable.

Kenya and the UK: the communities of Malindi Watamu and North Devon may be
35 thousands of kilometres apart with very different climates, but they share similar problems. Sea-level rise and erosion are eating into their beautiful coastlines, threatening the economy and people's livelihoods. Last year they decided to twin their biosphere reserves so as to join efforts and share expertise on how to adapt to a changing world.

Germany: the Rhön Biosphere Reserve has turned the art of local gastronomy into a
40 socio-economic success. Marketed under the 'Rhön umbrella brand' many products from the Biosphere Reserve are certified organic, meaning they have been grown without the use of standard pesticides or artificial fertilizers and without being genetically modified. All these Rhön products generate revenue for the entire region.

A recent project started by the MAB programme is the Biosphere Smart Initiative which
45 intends to maximize the use of new technologies to build a covenant for a sustainable future and a transition to green societies based on knowledge.

(*adapted from* http://www.unesco.org/new/en/natural-sciences/environment/
ecological-sciences/biosphere-reserves/biosphere-reserves-in-practice/)

[F] 0 The MAB Programme strives to …
☐ 1 Currently the World Network consists of …
☐ 2 The Network is developed in …
☐ 3 The solar power station in the Altaisky Biosphere Reserve will …
☐ 4 The Reka River has recently …
☐ 5 The Serra do Espinhaço Biosphere Reserve in Brazil …
☐ 6 The Jordan Biosphere Reserve …
☐ 7 By working together the two biosphere reserves in Kenya and the UK hope to …
☐ 8 The Rhön Biosphere Reserve in Germany …

A has contributed to the transition to green societies.
B 124 different countries.
C has introduced sound sustainable development practices.
D has been able to give work to people living in the area.
E learn from each other how best to cope with similar problems.
F ensure a liveable environment in the context of rapid environmental change.
G rewards communities which protect biodiversity and ecosystems.
H help to reduce the consumption of diesel fuel.
I 701 biosphere reserves.
J has helped to invigorate the marketing of local produce.
K become the object of a school project.

▶ *INVALSI Trainer*

Reading Comprehension 15
TASK Multiple Matching (Matching short texts)

TIPS AND STRATEGIES
- First read the questions. Try to paraphrase the statements. This will help you identify the answers.
- Quickly skim the text to try to understand the general meaning of the text.
- Read the questions again and predict which part of the text contains the answer.
- Scan the parts you think might contain the answer. If you find a possible answer, underline it.
- Check the questions again and mark the answer only if you think it is correct. If not, move on to other parts of the text and return to that question later.

Read the horoscopes for July, then choose the correct texts (A-F) to answer the questions (1-8). You can use a text more than once.

The first one (0) has been done for you.

July horoscopes

A ARIES – There's every reason to feel good about yourself. You've been working hard and now you find it much easier to reach for what you know you're capable of. Success at this stage has nothing to do with ambition. And now you know that the more you focus on what you really want, the more aware you'll be of your true strength.

B LEO – All of a sudden, you're going to start coming up with your best ideas. Pay attention to what your inner genius is encouraging you to do. Keep a notebook near and write down ideas and notions throughout the day. There is energy behind your thoughts and you will come up with solutions to problems that could turn out to be beneficial. It doesn't matter whether you feel creative, the fact is that you are innovative in a very practical way. Put that gift to use.

C VIRGO – Make room for a little chaos in your life. You love order and organization but sometimes it works against you. Pick a room, a table or some part of your space to calm down. Allow things to evolve in their own way. Use this period as a fermentation tank for your future objectives, desires, and plans. In all achievements there is a measure of chance, the unpredictable, and the unusual. Let both new ideas and opportunities in.

D CAPRICORN – This is a rich period for relationships. But you may feel the pressure to hold those that you meet at arm's length, never getting too close. Instead, make a point of letting down your guard and getting to know anyone who strikes your fancy without hesitation. People are drawn to something in you. Being open to receiving is one of your major life lessons.

58

E	AQUARIUS – The coming month is an excellent time to take a bit of space all for yourself again. You've been through a lot lately, so it would be wise to reassess. What's more, you will realise that your concerns were all in your imagination. There's no lack of things to do to keep yourself busy. It's time to give more importance to health and to minimize labour. And you'll be surprised to see how much you get done with little effort. Rest, recreation and repair are the keys to efficiency.	25 30
F	PISCES – Your financial life has a tendency to move in extreme cycles, more than that of most people you know. If you figure out how to ride the waves, you can do well for yourself. This is a period of wealth. It's great time to get into the habit of saving money and other valuables. The act of doing this will have a terrific effect – not just on your finances, but on your self-esteem.	 35

Which sign …

- [F] 0 is advised to put money aside?
- [ ] 1 has just come out of a difficult period of time?
- [ ] 2 should take note of all the ideas he have?
- [ ] 3 is giving too much importance to work?
- [ ] 4 should take advantage of new contacts?
- [ ] 5 now understands the importance of concentrating on specific goals?
- [ ] 6 is capable of finding concrete solutions?
- [ ] 7 tends to plan things well in advance?
- [ ] 8 has a strong power of attraction?

▶ INVALSI Trainer

Reading Comprehension 16
TASK Multiple Matching (Matching short texts)

> **TIPS AND STRATEGIES**
> Look at the whole text because the answers can be anywhere in the text and they do not come in order.

Read the reviews of different books, then choose the correct texts (A-F) to answer the questions (1-8). You can use a text more than once.

The first one (0) has been done for you.

Book recommendations for your summer

A Becky and Nicholas by Rachel T. Higgins

The fantasy I have been longing for – a breath of fresh air that holds the reader captive from the opening scene. Be warned, you will fall hard for Becky and Nicholas. You will swoon, you will gasp, you will laugh, and you will cry with a story that touches on all emotions. The characters and the reader are put in intense situations which will leave you on the edge of your seat. With impressive descriptions, impactful character development and a genuine style, this debut author will have you asking for more of her words.

B How to Be a Lion by Evelyne Hall

Leonard and Marianne are best friends. They talk on the phone every day (meow!) and spend all their free time together (napping and purring). But they have never actually met! Will they find a way? A great story of friendship that adults and teenagers will love. Vivid pictures and a refined layout will make this story a joy for your eyes, too. This story will give you a lot to think about today's world regarding how to take care of creatures, including humans, and the environment.

C Drawn Together by Suzanne Lang

A granddaughter and her grandmother – unable to converse – watch TV all day until the girl loses interest and turns to her violin. Grandmother then brings out her sketchbook and together they start 'talking' without words. They only use notes and colours, action and excitement. This is a delightfully simple story that explores communication problems between people who are so near and so distant at the same time. A unique story with amazing illustrations which tells a lot about communication between generations. It will surely be a hit with all ages.

D Aisha Unbound by Amal Saeda

Aisha is living a decent life in her village in Pakistan. She loves school and plans to go to college and become a teacher. But when she offends a member of the most influential family in the village, her dreams come to an end. As usual the author takes on challenging subjects – indentured servitude and the treatment of women – and makes them accessible to everyone while making the reader cheer for Aisha as she finds her way again.

60

E All Summer Long by Lynne Rie

A well-balanced book that shows one young Chinese girl's experience of settling in California with her family. Funny, imaginative, innovative, this book shows the difficulties of starting over in a new country in a way that you will soon be able to understand. A great book to open our eyes to the different and sometimes unseen ways people struggle and how we can make the world a better place just by being more inclusive and willing to listen to each other's stories. The stories we are told offer original and sweet insights on how to handle new experiences, make friends, and learn all sorts of fun things along the way.

F Legendary by Eileen Walton

This book of riddles is itself a kind of riddle composed with all the ingredients of a true classic novel. Magic, love, and loss permeate this stunning story which in the end takes the reader full circle to begin the tale again with fresh eyes. A charming mystery with a clever and resourceful protagonist.

Which book should you choose if ...

- [E] 0 you would like to experience how things can be seen differently from someone else's point of view?
- [ ] 1 brain teasers are your passion?
- [ ] 2 you would like to read a story about the power of art?
- [ ] 3 you enjoy stories about immigrants?
- [ ] 4 you have never read a fantasy novel?
- [ ] 5 books about the condition of women in different countries are of interest to you?
- [ ] 6 you would like to read a new author's first book?
- [ ] 7 stories whose protagonists are animals are your favourite kind?
- [ ] 8 you like graphic novels?

▶ *INVALSI Trainer*

Reading Comprehension 17
TASK Multiple Matching (Gap-fill)

TIPS AND STRATEGIES
The 'key' to this task is to know that each gap in the text can only be filled correctly by one of the sentences.

Read the text about how to access a flat.
Parts of the text have been removed. Choose the correct part (A-K) for each gap (1-8). There are two extra parts that you do not need to use. Write your answers in the spaces provided.

The first one (0) has been done for you.

Instructions for guests

Hi Sara!

You are all set to check in on Tuesday anytime after 4 p.m.! The front door code to 89 Marion Street, Brookline MA (0) ....C..... . The elevator entrance is located on the side of the building. The side door code is 8989*. Then push the button to open the door. You will be staying in flat 17, which is located on the first floor. The code to your flat (1) .... (include the # sign).

There's a common kitchen located on the 3rd floor if you wish (2) .... The equipment in the kitchen is easy to use. The manuals for the oven, dishwasher etc. can be found in the bottom drawer next to the sink.

Below is any additional information you may need during your stay. Please let me know if you have any questions at all.

Lock Instructions
To open: enter the access code into the keypad. (3) ...., a click will sound; immediately turn the lock to open the door.
To close: enter the access code and turn the lock away from the door.

Wi-Fi Information
Rooms are fully equipped with TV and Wi-Fi access. (4) ...., log onto the network 89 Marion Guest and enter the password maverickempire.

What to Bring
Here are some suggested 'check-list' items to bring with you or (5) ....:

- Coffee and coffee filters (4-cup size)
- Trash bags
- Paper products for the studio – Paper towels, napkins, etc. (Toilet paper will be replenished as needed during your stay)
- Cooking materials – Spices, condiments, oils, ingredients
- Additional toiletries – We provide travel size soap, shampoo and conditioner upon check-in. However, (6) ....
- Detergent and dryer sheets.

Laundry
There are coin operated washer and dryer machines located on the basement. Laundry (7) ....

Garden

Please clean the BBQ after every use. The cleaning utensils are located in the basement next to the laundry. If the gas runs out, please take it to a local petrol station, where you can simply swap it for a full tank.

A gardener will come and water the plants once a fortnight. Do not be alarmed if you see him, as he will let himself into the garden via the side gate. His name is Pedro.

Garbage

If you are staying short-term, you do not need to worry about the trash! Our cleaners will dispose of this for you upon your check-out. If you wish to dispose of trash during your stay, (8) .... The trash room is located in the basement of the building. There are large black barrels for garbage. Blue barrels are for recyclable goods. Failure to comply with the City of Brookline trash ordinance will result in fines of up to $250 per offense.

Parking Lot

Parking is available free of charge in some designated spaces. Do not park in the way of the electrical motorized gate when in a fully open or half way open position as it closes automatically after a few seconds. Do not leave any valuables inside your car while it is parked.

Departure Guidelines

Check out time is 11 a.m. The cleaning crew arrives at this time so please make sure that you have collected all personal belongings, have left the unit in the condition in which you found it, and have departed. Please let us know if there are any maintenance issues prior to check out. Before leaving, please switch off all the lights, lock all the windows and doors, strip the beds and place dirty bedding on the floor next to the bed.

Remember to give us a positive review – many thanks!

Last things

Parties are not allowed and smoking inside the property is forbidden. Also remember: no loud music or noise after 10 p.m. or before 7 a.m.

Best,

Alicia

A	After doing so
B	to do any cooking
C	is 8*192176
D	Please contact us immediately
E	to purchase shortly after you arrive
F	The building is a smoke-free environment
G	we recommend bringing your own as well
H	is #904209
I	To access Wi-Fi internet
J	here are the guidelines
K	is $2.50 cycle

▶ INVALSI Trainer

Reading Comprehension 18
TASK Multiple Matching (Gap-fill)

TIPS AND STRATEGIES
Be aware that you are looking for meaning and not for words. Paraphrasing and synonyms are used in many of the questions and if you were looking for words that exactly match those in the text, you won't find them. Instead, focus on ideas.

Read the text about an International Sand Sculpting Festival.
Parts of the text have been removed. Choose the correct part (A-K) for each gap (1-8). There are two extra parts that you do not need to use. Write your answers in the spaces provided.

The first one (0) has been done for you.

International Sand Sculpting Festival returns to Coronado Beach in San Diego, CA

Escape the city for the weekend without going too far with the 2018 San Diego Coronado Beach International Sand Sculpting Festival. See some of the world's best sand sculptors, who will (0) ....C.... . Two years ago the festival drew 1.5 million attendees, last year 2 million and this year's is sure to be a great success. The festival brings together more than 30 expert sand sculptors from as far away as Bulgaria, Poland, Russia, Italy and Portugal to compete for the grand prize.

64

Their creations, (1) ...., will no doubt impress. This year's theme is 'Celebrating Literacy', so sculptors will (2) .... The festival will feature sand-sculpting lessons and amusement-park rides for the kids. Food trucks and local vendors will (3) ...., and live entertainment
10 will enhance your experience. This year the festival will also (4) .... on Saturday night.

There are several options for getting to Coronado Island from San Diego: driving across the beautiful San Diego-Coronado Bridge, taking a ferry or water taxi across the Big Bay or driving across the seven-mile Silver Strand peninsula.

Where to eat near the festival

15 **Miguel's Cocina.** This Mexican eatery spills out onto the tiled courtyard of the Spanish-style 1902 El Cordova Hotel. Try (5) .... the famous jalapeño white sauce, or the grilled swordfish tacos.

MooTime Creamery. This local gathering spot is a must for dessert lovers seeking a tasty cool down. Try (6) .... chocolate chunks.

20 **Crown Room.** If (7) .... and looking for something to eat, Crown Room is a family-friendly restaurant with options that will appeal to the whole family, including local favourites like crab-stuffed prawns and freshly shucked oysters.

Primavera serves Italian typical dishes with huge portions and friendly service. Known for its Italian-style fresh fish plates, try (8) .... clam sauce.

A the black raspberry ice cream mixed with
B include a dazzling fireworks display
C put their amazing skills on full display
D favourites like linguine with
E honour the history and power of children's literature with their works
F you're hungry after the festival
G sell their wares and distribute free samples
H essential part of any beach trip
I made from just sand and water
J the shrimp burritos with
K you can't decide between seafood and Mexican

▶ INVALSI Trainer

Reading Comprehension 19
TASK Multiple Matching (Gap-fill)

B2

Read the article about parkour.
Parts of the text have been removed.
Choose the correct part (A-K) for each gap (1-8). There are two extra parts that you do not need to use. Write your answers in the spaces provided.

The first one (0) has been done for you.

What is parkour?

Parkour is one of the stand-out physical training movements of the 21st century. It involves of using all available urban surfaces and obstacles to (0) ….**C**…. while simultaneously keeping your movements fluid and simple. Practising parkour does not require special equipment or structures. Practitioners of the discipline are often referred to as *traceurs* or *traceuses*, and (1) …………, which Raymond Belle – the father of the 'father of parkour' David Belle – used to refer to all his numerous training methods, which were based on military obstacle courses, from climbing and running to jumping, balancing and more. Parkour (2) ………… soon after being created by David Belle in France in the late 1980s. The International Federation of the Art of Movement is the official federation for parkour worldwide. (3) …………, it is the official international association supporting the growth and accessibility of this groundbreaking transformative practice.

What follows is a list of the most common rules to follow if you want to practise parkour.

1 Progressive training is key

These days people only upload videos on YouTube showing really advanced moves. The thing is, as a beginner, you should start out by just admiring these moves; (4) ………… and slowly develop your mind and physical self. There are no shortcuts to parkour; it takes years of training to get where people like David Belle and Damien Walters are now. So take it slow.

2 Two are better than one

Regardless of whether you're doing basic moves or intermediate ones, always have someone with you who has done parkour for at least 2-3 months consistently every week. It's always better to (5) .... – you know, to analyze the situation, and to see if it's really feasible. I prefer to have at least 2 others (that means a total of 3 of us) around when I try something new.

3 How you dress can bring out the best and the worst in you

Dressing appropriately, or rather 'suiting up' for parkour is essential at the beginning. Always wear something light and that doesn't restrict your movement, which means jeans and jackets are not a good idea. Of course, one might say a *traceur* should be able to do parkour in anything they wear, but that can come later. Again, progressive training is key, (6) ...., and later on, once your basics and your foundation are strong, you can try training in other outfits like a business suit with a blazer and all that. Some people even train barefoot for the challenge.

4 Plan before you leap

Parkour is an individual sport. The difference with other sports like soccer and basketball is that you're interacting with inanimate objects, which means (7) .... Soccer and basketball involve other players which makes it harder to predict what might happen and can cause more serious injury. So plan before you leap – there's always a safer way around the obstacles you're facing.

5 (8) ....

And what if you get injured? Only resume practising once you're completely fine again. This is to prevent overusing your injured part and causing more injury to it than there already is. Furthermore, when you practise while you're still injured, you tend to avoid using the injured area so as to avoid pain. This will form bad habits which you will find hard to correct later. So take it slow, and be patient.

(*adapted from* http://parkour4mylife.blogspot.it/p/5-basic-parkour-rules.html)

A	gained worldwide visibility and became widespread
B	do parkour only after you've completely healed
C	go from one point to another in the least possible number of moves
D	start with light clothes and running shoes
E	always train in pairs
F	the word 'parkour' actually derives from the French word *parcours*
G	just start from the basics
H	you can predict what might happen
I	walk first, then run
J	get a second opinion before trying out something new
K	founded by the leading global parkour communities and pioneers of the discipline

▶ INVALSI Trainer

Reading Comprehension 20
TASK Multiple Matching (Gap-fill)

Read the text about the art of fresco painting.
Parts of the text have been removed. Choose the correct part (A-K) for each gap (1-8).
There are two extra parts that you do not need to use. Write your answers in the spaces provided.

The first one (0) has been done for you.

The art of fresco painting and the mission to keep this tradition

Once upon a time, vibrant frescoes adorned the walls and ceilings of churches and noble residences in Europe. The fresco is celebrated as (0) ....C.... . Though most commonly associated with the art of the Italian Renaissance, the painting technique has been around for millennia, inspiring ancient and contemporary artists alike. Created by painting directly
5 onto plaster, (1) .... Unsurprisingly, muralists favour this durability, as illustrated by well-preserved masterpieces including the Roman wall paintings of Pompeii and Renaissance artist Michelangelo's world-famous Sistine Chapel ceiling.

Today (2) .... Fortunately, a Florentine master by the name of Lorenzo Giani is fighting to keep this extraordinary technique alive. A classically trained architect, (3) .... At the
10 turn of the last century, his great-uncle owned a sculpting and painting *bottega* in Florence until 1926. After WWII he left Italy, never to return. (4) .... and eventually learned fresco painting from several well-known masters. Today he is sharing his knowledge through informative workshops and public demonstrations.

In today's eco-conscious world, (5) .... This being said, there is a limited number
15 of pigments allotted for creating colours. Lorenzo's goal is to unite his knowledge of architecture with his passion for art to implement frescoes in modern interior design.

A fresco painting is a work of wall or ceiling art created by applying (6) .... Its title comes from 'fresh' in Italian, as a true fresco's intonaco is wet when the paint is applied. There are three common types of fresco: *buon*, *secco* and *mezzo*. To paint a *buon* ('true')
20 fresco, an artist paints directly onto freshly mixed plaster. Due to the natural tack of the wet intonaco, the pigment used to paint a *buon* fresco does not need to contain a binding medium; instead, it can simply be mixed with water. Instead, a *secco* ('dry') fresco employs dry plaster as its canvas. To make the paint stick to the plaster, the pigments must be mixed with a binding medium, such as a glue adhesive or egg yolk. A *mezzo* ('medium') fresco is
25 painted onto nearly dry *intonaco*.

The best method, *buon* fresco, involves painting on a thin layer of wet plaster. The plaster reacts with the air while drying, causing a chemical reaction. Pigments are then affixed to the plaster's surface in a protective crystalline crust. This is why so many frescoes have withstood the test of time, lasting several decades, if not centuries. Naturally, the durability
30 of a fresco depends on many factors such as weather conditions and location. (7) ...., which may prove challenging for beginners. Depending on the type of plaster, drying times can vary between two and five hours. For this reason, (8) ....

Lorenzo uses the same exact techniques and materials once employed by Renaissance masters. Morning demonstrations are offered in Lorenzo's spacious studio which is to be
35 found in an iconic courtyard in the historical centre of Florence just behind the Uffizi. Participants will complete and take home a small fresco that they paint themselves. For those interested in attending an actual workshop, please contact Lorenzo directly. He also does portraiture on fresco via private commission.

68

A this tradition has all but faded into irrelevance
B a large composition like a wall mural must be done in small sections
C one of the most significant mural-making techniques in the history of art
D pigment onto *intonaco*, or a thin layer of plaster
E many works of well-preserved wall art discovered by archaeologists
F frescoes offer a permanence not found in other forms of art
G Lorenzo decided to follow his artistic dreams
H the artist must complete the painting before the plaster dries
I painted on dry plaster, this piece is a *secco* fresco
J fresco painting is a wonderful opportunity for those seeking natural and organic materials
K Lorenzo's passion and talent for art runs in his blood

▶ INVALSI Trainer

Reading Comprehension 21
TASK Multiple Matching (Gap-fill)

B2

TIPS AND STRATEGIES
- Always read the whole text first. Then start again and read up to the first gap and the sentence immediately after it.
- The sentences before and after each gap are particularly important as the most relevant information is usually there.
- Sometimes there isn't a clue in the sentence immediately before or after the gap. That's why you really need to read the whole text to get its meaning – sometimes the 'clue' is the entire paragraph.
- You don't have to start with the first gap – start with the one you think is going to be the easiest and leave the hardest for later, when you'll have fewer options to choose between.

**Read the information about the benefits of team sports for young people.
Choose the correct sentence (1-8) to summarize each paragraph (A-G).
There are two extra sentences that you do not need to use. Write your answers in the spaces provided.**

The first one (0) has been done for you.

Why are team sports important for young people?

Team sports give more than just physical benefits. Participating in team sports influences a young person's future by building his/her awareness of teamwork and cooperation, responsibility and by helping him/her make new friends. There are physiological as well as mental benefits.

5   Here are just a few of the many benefits that participating in a team sport can give you.

   A ....

   A high five, pat on the back, thumbs up, or even a nod of approval – these are simple gestures that can help build confidence. You'll often see these signals come from teammates and coaches when they want to recognize someone for a job well done. By being part of a
10 team, you will give and receive praise. Receiving recognition from a team mate or a coach will be important as you have been acknowledged for your efforts. And as you are praised for your efforts, you will become more confident.

   B ....

   You may think that the decisions you take only affect you, but as it turns out, that simply
15 isn't true! Team sports teach you about a sense of belonging to something bigger than yourself. When you play sports on a team, you quickly learn that every choice you make has an impact on your teammates and on your opponents, too! The ability to work well with others is a skill that you will bring with you throughout your entire life. It will prove to be beneficial when you have to work with others at their jobs.

20 **C** ....

   Playing on a team will show you how essential and, on some occasions, unique your role on the team is. You will learn that what really matters is not who is the best or on top; you must learn to be accountable for individual actions and to become a role model of sportsmanship.

70

D ....

25 Making choices can often take time. But the truth is we usually tend to overcomplicate very simple decisions. Playing team sports will teach you to think things over and come to a decision at a quicker pace than you might experience in your everyday life. As a bonus, making quick decisions can help develop a sense of self-confidence that you may not readily develop otherwise.

30 **E** ....

Because of the social aspect of team sports, you'll learn how to behave in social situations. You'll soon develop a sense of community, while maintaining and developing stronger bonds with your teammates.

F   _0_

35 There will be times in life that you may have to settle for being second-best for the greater good. This can feel like defeat if you don't realize that there is often more at play than you can initially see. Sometimes the most gratifying choice you can make is the one to help someone else even when it is not what you would like to do. Learning mutual understanding and self-sacrifice is a lesson you will certainly carry throughout the course
40 of your life!

G ....

It's always exciting to win in life. But sometimes the greater lessons come from your failures. If you play on a team for any amount of time, it is highly likely that you will experience a fair share of losses. Each of these losses are an opportunity for you to learn about moving
45 on and trying again!

Team sports ...

0   can teach you to put others first.
1   can teach you to be decisive.
2   help you keep fit.
3   develop self-esteem.
4   teach leadership skills.
5   teach respect.
6   can teach you about the bigger picture.
7   can teach you to bounce back.
8   help develop stronger relationships.

▶ INVALSI Trainer

Reading Comprehension 22
TASK Multiple Choice Questions

Read the text about the Community Rules and Regulations, then choose the correct answer (A, B, C or D) for questions 1-8.
Only one answer is correct.

The first one (0) has been done for you.

Community rules and regulations

While you are here, have fun and be considerate of the natural and serene atmosphere that helps make our island the perfect place to visit all year round. We respectfully request that all residents and guests observe the following regulations to ensure a more pleasant stay.

- Beach towels and beach items such as coolers, toys, boogie boards, etc. should be kept out of sight of adjoining properties, golf courses, and roadways. Toys and bikes should be parked near the residence or in garages, and not left on lawns or driveways or on beach walks.

- Exterior lights for oceanside properties: take care that lights do not shine onto the beach during loggerhead turtle nesting season (May-October) to protect young hatchlings who are drawn to the light.

- Trash cans and recycling bins should be kept in designated service yards where they will be picked up by the refuse service on the designated days. Please keep garbage in trash cans to discourage animals from spreading trash.

- Daytime parking on roads cannot impede emergency vehicles, driveways or leisure trail access. No parking is allowed on primary streets, while overnight parking and beach parking is prohibited on all roads. Please park on your driveway.

- Motorcycles and motorized scooters are not permitted. Trailers and commercially marked vehicles may not remain outdoors overnight and must be garaged.

- Roller blades, roller skates and skate boards shall not be allowed on the walking paths, sidewalks and roadways.

- Golf carts are operated only by properly licensed drivers and in public areas used by motor vehicles. No golf carts can carry more persons than can be properly seated in the vehicle. If on the roads after dark, golf carts must have properly functioning headlights and taillights.

- Pets must be leashed at all times when outdoors, except as permitted on the beach during certain times of the year. We also ask that you please clean up after your pets and dispose of waste properly. On the dog owners' property, when outside the home, dogs are kept either on a leash or properly enclosed within a fenced area at all times.

- For your safety please do not feed any wildlife, especially fish and alligators. The latter are wild and dangerous animals and extreme caution should be taken when near them.

- Property owners and renters shall not place any object such as automobiles, garbage cans, material to be recycled, brush, grass clippings, leaves or other yard debris or rubbish on property not owned by themselves or their landlord without permission.

- Please be a courteous neighbour and be mindful of noise levels of people and pets.

- Guest passes must be displayed prominently in your vehicle while on the island.

INVALSI Trainer

- Texting while driving is not allowed in the whole area. Remember to respect speed limits too.

40
- To protect the privacy rights of residents and visitors, drones may be operated only with the written permission of each property owner over which the craft flies.

- Absolutely no charcoal grilling, or other types of open fire on porches, decks, patios, or landings above ground level. Only cook/grill on ground level. Strictly enforced by the police. Electric and gas grills are permitted only if permanently attached to landing and not covered by any type of roof or awning.

0 **The Community Rules and Regulations apply to …**
- [ ] A visitors only.
- [ ] B people living here.
- [ ] C beach goers.
- [X] D everyone.

1 **If you have a bicycle you …**
- [ ] A cannot ride it on the beach during the day.
- [ ] B should always lock it when you leave it unattended.
- [ ] C are requested to keep it in your garage when you are not using it.
- [ ] D must wear a helmet when riding it.

2 **Exterior lights …**
- [ ] A should be left on when you are at home.
- [ ] B can be turned off when you leave.
- [ ] C are prohibited as they cause problems to animals.
- [ ] D must be off in summer for houses facing the sea.

3 **Garbage …**
- [ ] A must be kept in specific areas.
- [ ] B is collected every day.
- [ ] C should be disposed of individually.
- [ ] D can be kept in your yard or garden.

4 **Parking is allowed …**
- [ ] A anywhere only at night.
- [ ] B on your private property.
- [ ] C along the main roads during the day.
- [ ] D near the beachwalk all day long.

5 **It is prohibited to …**
- [ ] A ride a motorbike on the island.
- [ ] B move around in a trailer or a caravan.
- [ ] C park commercial vehicles near the beach.
- [ ] D visit the island by bicycle.

6 **If you have a dog …**
- [ ] A check which beaches let pets in.
- [ ] B be aware that it is prohibited to walk it on the beach.
- [ ] C it must be kept in your garden or indoors.
- [ ] D always keep it on a leash when walking it around.

7 **Local wildlife includes …**
- [ ] A poisonous animals.
- [ ] B some endangered species.
- [ ] C rare species of birds.
- [ ] D dangerous animals.

8 **If you want to have access to the island …**
- [ ] A you need a permanent pass.
- [ ] B you must be a resident.
- [ ] C a pass is required.
- [ ] D an ID has to be produced.

▶ INVALSI Trainer

Reading Comprehension 23

TASK Multiple Choice Questions

B2

Read an article about problems people have daily with maths, then choose the correct answer (A, B, C or D) for questions 1-7. Only one answer is correct.

The first one (0) has been done for you.

Millions 'struggling' with maths

Millions of adults in the UK could be missing out on the benefits of improved numeracy skills due to a failure to appreciate their importance in everyday life, according to a survey released for National Numeracy Day.

Being bad at maths should no longer be seen as a 'badge of honour' or down to genetics, according to National Numeracy, an organization which aims to challenge the nation's negative view of the subject. National Numeracy is highlighting the life-long value that greater skills and confidence with numeracy can bring and encouraging people to take action to brush up on their numbers know-how.

Rachel Riley, mathematician and TV presenter, is an official ambassador for National Numeracy and commented: 'Good numeracy isn't about being a maths whiz or having the ability to do complex mental arithmetic; it's about having the knowledge and confidence to apply numbers-based solutions to everyday tasks such as shopping, budgeting, planning a trip or even following a recipe. With numbers playing such a key role in all our lives it's vital that people not only start to view it as an essential skill, but also one to be proud of. Whatever your current ability, numeracy is a skill you can improve on at any age.'

Chris Humphries, chairman of National Numeracy, said that poor numeracy skills can 'blight' an individual's life, leaving them at a higher risk of being excluded from school or out of work as an adult. Figures from a government survey, published last year, show that 17 million adults in England have basic maths skills that are, at best, the same as an 11-year-old's. The Skills for Life survey, which questioned 7,000 16- to 65-year-olds, showed that almost half of the working age population has numeracy skills roughly the same as those expected of primary school children, and the proportion has risen (from 47% to 49%) in the last eight years. Speaking at the launch of National Numeracy, Mr Humphries, former chief executive of the UK Commission for Employment and Skills, said: 'That's a scary figure, because what it means is they often can't understand deductions on their payslip, they often can't calculate or give change. They have problems with timetables, they are certainly going to have problems with tax and even with interpreting graphs, charts and metres that are necessary for their jobs. It does matter, poor numeracy seriously blights an individual's life chances.'

Mike Ellicock, chief executive of National Numeracy, said: "We want to challenge this 'I can't do maths' attitude that is prevalent in the UK," adding that it was vital that all primary school teachers understand key maths concepts, as young children who fail to learn the basics will suffer later on. "For my money, Key Stage 1 (five to seven-year-olds) is the crucial area. There has been talk about having specialist maths teachers in Years 5 and 6, but my view is Key Stage 1 is crucial, and if you look at children and young adults that struggle with maths later in their lives, you can pretty quickly trace it back to the ideas that they met in Key Stage 1."

A YouGov poll of 2,068 adults, commissioned by National Numeracy, reveals that while four in five (80%) would feel embarrassed to tell someone they were bad at reading and writing, just more than half (56%) would feel embarrassed about saying the same of their maths skills.

TIPS AND STRATEGIES
- Read the question and all the options. Never choose an answer without reading them all!
- Cross out incorrect options immediately to prevent confusion.
- Once you have chosen the answer, check to see if all the information it gives is backed up by the text.

0 What is National Numeracy's objective?
- [ ] A To get more investments in education.
- [ ] B They intend to promote numeracy in schools.
- [X] C They aim at a change in the UK's attitude to maths.
- [ ] D To change maths teaching methods, especially in primary school.

1 How do you interpret the word 'blight' (line 31)?
- [ ] A Harm.
- [ ] B Influence.
- [ ] C Have an impact on.
- [ ] D Help.

2 How many adults have low maths skills?
- [ ] A 7 million.
- [ ] B 17 million.
- [ ] C Half the population.
- [ ] D The data is not given.

3 What do low numeracy skills prevent you from doing?
- [ ] A Reading the local newspaper.
- [ ] B Using a calculator.
- [ ] C Using a credit card.
- [ ] D Interpreting data.

4 What does the text suggest about improving maths at an early age?
- [ ] A Starting to learn maths at the age of seven.
- [ ] B Teaching key maths concepts to all primary school teachers.
- [ ] C Hiring specialist maths teachers for Key Stage 1.
- [ ] D Hiring specialist maths teachers in Years 5 and 6.

5 When should basic numeracy skills start being taught?
- [ ] A At 7.
- [ ] B At 5.
- [ ] C At 6.
- [ ] D At 10.

6 Which situation is the least embarrassing for an adult according to a YouGov poll?
- [ ] A Admitting you have low maths skills.
- [ ] B Admitting you have low literacy skills.
- [ ] C Not being able to give change.
- [ ] D Not being able to understand deductions on a payslip.

7 What kind of data is the article based on?
- [ ] A Data collected through international surveys.
- [ ] B Data given by UK associations.
- [ ] C Data collected among primary school teachers.
- [ ] D Data from governmental surveys.

▶ INVALSI Trainer

Reading Comprehension 24
TASK Multiple Choice Questions

Read a text about the gender gap in education, then choose the correct answer (A, B, C or D) for questions 1-7. Only one answer is correct.

The first one (0) has been done for you.

Closing the gender gap

Gender equality is at the heart of human rights. Women's empowerment is central to reducing poverty, promoting development and addressing the world's most urgent challenges. Figures show that if every country boosted the number of women in the workplace to match the progress toward gender parity of its fastest-improving neighbour,
5   global GDP could increase by $12 trillion within a decade.

It has been widely demonstrated that educated women improve the health and well-being of their families and communities. Giving girls access to quality education is crucial to realizing a more equal world. Historically, women have had lower levels of education than men all around the world. Although the educational attainment of women has grown
10   at a quicker pace than that of men in many parts of the world since the mid-20th century, the situation is not the same in all countries. In fact, recent research has shown that 16 million girls aged 6 to 11 will never start school. That is twice the number of boys.

Unfinished business

By 2014, 88% of girls of primary school age (about 6 to 11 year-olds) were enrolled
15   in school globally. The most evident increase was seen in sub-Saharan Africa. Meanwhile, the out-of-school rate for girls declined from 18% in 2000 to 10% in 2014. The rate of boys out of school declined from 12% to 9%.

But the data also point to a still-unmet demand for primary education. Of the 136 million children who began primary school in 2014, 38 million will leave school before reaching
20   the last grade. In sub-Saharan Africa and southern Asia, where most of these children live, early gains between 2000 and 2007 are now at risk of being reversed. Poverty, isolation and inequality are barriers that require more targeted policy solutions.

Universal secondary education presents new challenges

The provision of quality secondary education by 2030 will also require more innovative
25   solutions, such as 'second chance' education and vocational training, to enable youth to acquire the skills they need to contribute to economic growth. Young adolescents, roughly between the ages of 12 to 14, comprise 16% of the global out-of-school population and are twice as likely to be excluded compared to children younger than 12. Youth (roughly 15 to 17 year-olds) comprise 37% of the out-of-school population. They are less likely to have had
30   any exposure to schooling based on the out-of-school rate from a decade ago.

What are the prospects for adolescent girls?

While the male and female out-of-school rates are very similar at the global level, this is not the case at the regional level. In sub-Saharan Africa and South and West Asia, where most of these out-of-school young people live, females are more likely to be excluded from
35   education. In West Asia, for example, 20% of adolescent girls of lower secondary school age are out of school compared to 13% of boys. In sub-Saharan Africa, the female rate is 36% compared to 32% for males.

76

Ensuring quality education and learning

The demand is growing for more and better data that can shed further light on those
40 who are excluded from education and learning. To support countries confronting ever more complex challenges, such as the measurement of learning and equity, it is important to develop a new generation of indicators to help countries make informed decisions that will improve the education and learning prospects of all children and youth.

---

0 What does the verb 'boost' (line 3) mean?

- [ ] A Lift.
- [ ] B Encourage.
- [X] C Raise.
- [ ] D Top.

1 Why is gender equality important to economic development?

- [ ] A It can also lead to health improvements.
- [ ] B It is related to important improvements in life expectancy.
- [ ] C It stimulates economic growth.
- [ ] D All individuals can reach at least a basic minimum level of skills.

2 Which part of the world saw the largest decrease in the out-of-school rate?

- [ ] A Europe.
- [ ] B Sub-Saharan Africa.
- [ ] C North America.
- [ ] D South America.

3 What does the sentence '38 million will leave school before reaching the last grade' (line 19) mean?

- [ ] A All the children who entered primary education in 2014 will complete it.
- [ ] B Not all the children who entered primary education in 2014 will complete it.
- [ ] C More and more children have entered primary education since 2014.
- [ ] D There are still a few children who don't complete primary education.

4 Who is likely not to 'have had any exposure to schooling based on the out-of-school rate from a decade ago' (line 29)?

- [ ] A 15- to 17-year-olds.
- [ ] B 12- to 14-year-olds.
- [ ] C Girls.
- [ ] D Boys.

5 Which of the following could be a summary of the text?

- [ ] A Out-of-school rates are decreasing all around the world.
- [ ] B Girls are closing the gender gap in out-of-school rates at global level, but inequalities persist.
- [ ] C There are still too many young people who have had no exposure to schooling at all.
- [ ] D In some areas of the world too many young people are at a high risk of leaving school early.

6 What still prevents children in some parts of the world from regularly going to school?

- [ ] A Lack of qualified teachers.
- [ ] B Living long distances from school.
- [ ] C Health problems.
- [ ] D Poverty and isolation.

7 What kind of information does the text provide?

- [ ] A Mainly factual information.
- [ ] B Factual information and opinions.
- [ ] C Factual information and some definitions.
- [ ] D Only factual information.

▶ *INVALSI Trainer*

Reading Comprehension 25
TASK Multiple Choice Questions

Read the review of Jane Goodall's book 'In the Shadow of Man', then choose the correct answer (A, B, C or D) for questions 1-7. Only one answer is correct.

The first one (0) has been done for you.

Jane Goodall, 'In the Shadow of Man'

Jane Goodall is known for her observational work with chimpanzees. 'In the Shadow of Man' is a highly interesting read
5 for anyone who has ever wanted to know more about her work, and the nature of chimpanzees in general. Written in 1971, the book is accessible and not full
10 of scientific jargon.

'In the Shadow of Man' tells the story of when Goodall began her research at the Gombe Stream Reserve in Africa, and how
15 she slowly built a relationship with the chimps that, in turn, began to build one with her. She discusses how she not only had to earn their trust, but also
20 what she observed as far as their habits and behaviours are concerned. The straightforward and engaging, even humorous, tone makes this animal study
25 read almost like a novel. As Goodall describes the exploits of the group of chimps she would end up studying for years, you find yourself growing attached
30 to the animals along with her as you see their distinct personalities emerge. More importantly, Goodall makes a compelling case for the reader
35 to recognize the need for protective measures to be taken to preserve the chimpanzees and their habitat. Readers will

learn about David Graybeard,
40 the first chimp that allowed Goodall to approach him, as well as Mike, Goliath, Leakey, Mr McGregor, Worzle, Goblin, among many others. While
45 anyone reading that list would think they were mere names and that is all, Goodall actually manages to develop the chimps' characters within the book. And
50 although chimps do not have as distinct facial characteristics as do humans, the book is filled with facial photographs of these chimps, and I continually found
55 myself thumbing through to see the actual face of the chimp she was speaking about.

One aspect Goodall speaks about is animal testing. Although
60 she does not state that she is completely against it, she views the ways in which labs (and even the zoo) house the chimps as almost 'criminal' in her opinion.
65 Laboratories often like to keep chimps housed in small cages, leaving them with nothing to do all day except wait around for the next painful experiment.
70 Chimps are at their best when they are free to climb. Because these are highly intelligent creatures, over time they can become depressed and lethargic
75 – just as a human would if kept in a small prison cell.

Personally, after having read her book, I agree with what she says. This is not to imply that
80 I think scientific experiments should all together be abandoned, but one is really forced to think twice about the poor ways in which the
85 animals are treated. Hopefully, there will come a time when experimenting on higher animals won't be needed. The biggest difference between
90 them and us is that they have not been able to learn speech, but they have shown that they do have an awareness of self – probably far more than
95 we realize.

'In the Shadow of Man' is a terrific book. Goodall is not only a revered primatologist, but an excellent writer as well.
100 Her story reads almost like a memoir, richly descriptive, but at the same time full of technical observations on chimpanzee behaviour. Since reading this
105 book, and having contemplated the great apes, I view human beings differently.

Recommended for all humans.

*(adapted from
http://themoderatevoice.com/
book-review-in-the-shadow-
of-man-by-jane-goodall/)*

INVALSI Trainer

TIPS AND STRATEGIES
- If two of the options mean the same thing but use different words, they are BOTH incorrect.
- If only part of the information is correct, that answer choice is incorrect.
- An option that is too broad is incorrect.

---

0 What does Jane Goodall do for a living?
- [X] A She studies primates.
- [ ] B She's a novelist.
- [ ] C She teaches at university.
- [ ] D She's a journalist.

1 What is 'In the Shadow of Man' about?
- [ ] A Animal testing.
- [ ] B Scientific experiments on chimpanzees in Africa.
- [ ] C The observation of chimpanzees in their natural habitat.
- [ ] D A woman and her relationship with chimpanzees.

2 What does the phrase 'and that is all' (line 47) **mean in this context?**
- [ ] A The list of names is complete.
- [ ] B The names on the list are not all the chimps she met.
- [ ] C It's something more than a list of names.
- [ ] D The names on the list are all we need to know.

3 According to the author, what is wrong with animal testing?
- [ ] A Animals are kept in small cages and may become depressed.
- [ ] B Animals may die during the experiments.
- [ ] C Animals are underfed and ill-treated.
- [ ] D Animals are free to move around the lab.

4 What does the sentence "'In the Shadow of Man' is a terrific book" (line 96) **mean?**
- [ ] A The book is full of terrible stories.
- [ ] B The book is extremely good.
- [ ] C Some of the photos in the book are cruel.
- [ ] D It's a book about terrible actions against animals.

5 Why is the book 'recommended for all humans' (line 108)?
- [ ] A Because men and chimpanzees have a lot in common.
- [ ] B Because it is easy to read.
- [ ] C Because we can understand what is wrong with animal testing.
- [ ] D Because it teaches us a lot about both men and animals.

6 What kind of book is 'In the Shadow of Man'?
- [ ] A A biography.
- [ ] B A novel.
- [ ] C A journal.
- [ ] D An autobiography.

7 The book is intended for …
- [ ] A children.
- [ ] B the general public.
- [ ] C the academic world.
- [ ] D scientists only.

▶ INVALSI Trainer

Language Practice 1

TASK A Underline the right option.

Vitamin D is an essential nutrient for good health, but it seems that many Americans (1) *are taking / take / took* too much. Between 2007 and 2008, only 0.2 percent of Americans were exceeding the upper limit of vitamin D. In 2014, that number jumped to (2) *a / the / –* three percent of Americans.
(3) *Although / However / Because* many of us believe that if something is good for you, you should just take more of it, that is not the case when it (4) *deals with / comes to / is up to* vitamin D. One study claims that excessive vitamin D (5) *would / can / should* lead to calcium build up in the blood.

Score: .... /5

TASK B Change the form of the words in brackets to complete the sentences correctly.

1 She was almost .... (RECOGNIZE) with that new haircut.
2 They had to try an entirely .... (DIFFER) approach.
3 Her latest .... (PUBLISH) is about the first man on the Moon.
4 Not everyone expressed their .... (APPROVE) of the management's decision.
5 .... (FORTUNE), my train has just been cancelled. I am so cross.

Score: .... /5

TASK C Complete the following sentences with a question tag.

1 You don't know where he got the information from, ... ?
2 You've no idea where my sister is, ... ?
3 You wouldn't happen to know how much he's spent, ... ?
4 You couldn't tell me when they'll be back, ... ?
5 You won't tell me when the bank closes, ... ?

Score: .... /5

TASK D Put the paragraphs in the correct order.

Refugee team competes in World Athletics Championships

☐ A Ahmed Bashir Farah, Anjelina Lohalith, Dominic Lobalu, Rose Lokonyen and Kadar Omar and they will be participating as members of the Athlete Refugee Team.

☐ B 'I feel great going to London,' he said. 'We only have a few days left. I want to run my best time and qualify for the next stage. You know this is my first big international race so it's normal, you have to feel a little nervous and scared but once I'm on the field, the fear will leave me.'

☐ C Five refugee athletes are heading to London from Kenya to compete in the World Athletics Championships opening this week, the first time in the competition's 34-year history that refugees will be taking part. Their names are:

☐ D Nineteen-year-old Ahmed, who will compete in the 800 metres, has been a refugee in Nairobi since he fled violence in Somalia with his mother and two sisters when he was just nine years old.

☐ E The athletes are pleased to have the opportunity to compete internationally after months of training in the Kenyan capital, Nairobi.

(*adapted from* http://www.unhcr.org/)

Score: .... /5

Total score: .... /20

80

Language Practice 2

TASK A Complete the text with the phrases below. There are three extra phrases.

as • being • have a habit of • like • to be • highest • a • worth of • most • spending • the • over • ever

We all have unforgettable moments we want to keep with us forever. For me (1) .... of these moments revolve around my travels. (2) .... the time I went to New York in winter, as I wanted to ice-skate at The Rink at Rockefeller Center. With room for only 150 skaters at (3) .... time, I will never forget the intimate, incredible experience of that winter day in New York City. Or I still remember (4) .... ten days climbing Mt Kilimanjaro to stand proudly on the (5) .... point in Africa.
I now have ten years and over 35 countries (6) .... cherished memories, each moment having shaped my life along the way. But the thousands of photographs I accumulate (7) .... fading away in the 'cloud', and I tend to forget that they're sitting there saved. So I've started to favour print (8) .... pixels, because these moments deserve (9) .... printed, and nothing will (10) .... beat holding a physical photo book in your hands.

Score: .... /5

TASK B Change the form of the words in brackets to complete the sentences correctly.

1. My grandfather knew everything about the old village and its .... (INHABIT).
2. Why are you so convinced that their discovery will be so .... (REVOLUTION)?
3. Susie hadn't realized that he had come back, and was shocked at his sudden .... (APPEAR).
4. In the introduction you should provide a clear .... (EXPLAIN) of the objectives of your project.
5. It was clear the theory could not be explained .... (SCIENCE).

Score: .... /5

TASK C This is a job interview. Match the questions with the appropriate answer. There is one extra question.

☐ 1 What is your greatest strength?
☐ 2 What is your greatest weakness?
☐ 3 What are your salary expectations?
☐ 4 How do you handle stress and pressure?
☐ 5 Why do you want this job?
☐ 6 What are your goals for the future?

A Once I gain additional experience, I would like to move on from a technical position to management.
B I would like to be compensated fairly for my experience.
C I used to leave assignments until the last minute, but then I learned to schedule my time very effectively.
D When I'm working on a project, I don't want just to meet deadlines. Rather, I prefer to complete the project well ahead of schedule. Last year, I even earned a bonus for completing a report one week ahead of time.
E This job is a good fit for what I've been doing and enjoying throughout my career. It offers a mix of short-term projects and long-term goals.

Score: .... /5

TASK D Underline the right option.

Food plays a big role in your life (1) *but / so that / because* you need it to survive. (2) *Unfortunately / Anyway / But*, not all foods are good for you. Junk food is a group of foods that is high in calories, low in nutrients and usually contains harmful synthetic ingredients. Most junk foods are processed foods; (3) *for example / thus / however*, they are no longer in their natural state. (4) *So / Therefore / In addition*, they are stripped of certain essential nutrients. Finally, junk food is usually high in calories. Your body does not like to waste energy; (5) *therefore / but / because* the excessive calories are usually stored as fat, causing weight gain.

(adapted from http://energyfanatics.com/2008/06/15/why-junk-food-bad/)

Score: .... /5

Total score: .... /20

▶ INVALSI Trainer

Language Practice 3 B1

TASK A Underline the right option.

Coeliac disease (CD) (1) *was caused / caused / is caused* by an immune response to gluten proteins. Its rate of diagnosis is increasing in European countries. (2) *However, / Since / Because* its true prevalence is considered (3) *many great / much greater / great* than what is currently clinically diagnosed and is estimated (4) *being / be / to be* between 3% and 10% of the population. The only current remedy for those suffering (5) *from / of / for* CD is the total removal of gluten from their diet.
To ensure the safety of those people, (6) *– / the / a* current EU legislation requires products (7) *to make / making / make* a 'gluten free' claim (8) *containing / contain / to contain* less than 20 mg/kg of gluten. (9) *Thanks to / Due to / In spite of* the possibility of low level contamination, risk assessment relies (10) *on / in / for* the measurement of gluten levels in raw ingredients and the final processed 'gluten free' product.

(*adapted from* https://ec.europa.eu/)

Score: .... /5

TASK B Change the form of the words in brackets to complete the sentences correctly.

1 Unfortunately there are places where young people are .... (ABLE) to find jobs.
2 Our .... (FRIEND) goes back to when we were at university together.
3 She has an intriguing smile and a lovely .... (PERSON).
4 The .... (RELATE) between the two countries is not improving.
5 During the party she kept smiling .... (NERVE).

Score: .... /5

TASK C Complete the conversation with the phrases below. There are two extra phrases.

I'm afraid you can't • I think I can manage • do you mind if • sure, go ahead • I'm sorry but • thanks a lot • do you think I could

S: Dr Sanders, (1)..................... I go home in the afternoon?
Dr S: (2)..................... . Are you feeling OK?
S: I'm fine but I've got a lot to do: I'm moving into my new house at the end of the month. (3)..................... take tomorrow morning off as well?
Dr S: No, (4)..................... . I've arranged a meeting with our Marketing Office tomorrow morning.
S: Oh, yes. I'd forgotten.
Dr S: What about taking some holiday next week?
S: No, thanks. (5)..................... . I'll need to take some holiday later.

Score: .... /5

TASK D Put the paragraphs in the correct order.

State of the world's children

Every child has the right to health, education and protection, and every society has a stake in expanding children's opportunities in life. Yet,

☐ A great progress in school enrolment in many parts of the world, the number of children aged 6 to 11 who are out of school has increased since 2011.

☐ B Around the world, children make up nearly half of the almost 900 million people living on less than US$1.90 a day. Their families

☐ C around the world, millions of children are denied a fair chance for no reason other than the country, gender or circumstances into which they are born.

☐ D struggle to afford the basic health care and nutrition needed to provide them with a strong start. These deprivations leave a lasting imprint. Despite

☐ E About 124 million children and adolescents do not attend school, and two out of five leave primary school without basic skills, according to 2013 data.

This challenge is compounded by the increasingly protracted nature of armed conflict.

(*adapted from* http://www.un.org/en/)

Score: .... /5

Total score: .... /20

82

Language Practice 4

INVALSI Trainer

 B1

TASK A Underline the right option.

Is NASA Florida worth (1) *to visit / visit / visiting*? We are going to Disney World for a week, and (2) *are thinking about visiting / are planning a visit / are considering to visit* NASA for a day. We have two young kids, eight and five years old. Please advise, many thanks.
Jane

We (3) *were going / went / had been* there some years ago and loved it. It was amazing and very interesting. However, if your family members aren't much into space, then it (4) *probably is to / might / will* be one to miss.
If you decide to go, (5) *you will be / you are / be sure* to get there early since it takes about one hour to get there from the Disney area. To visit NASA Florida you'll have to book a tour. A part of the tour is by bus. There are about four stops and the busses run regularly. This is what we spent most of the day (6) *doing / to do / done*, visiting one area, then taking the bus to another area and so on. We also enjoyed the IMAX theater and (7) *to look / looking / look* at the rocket garden. We are a large family with three teens and three children under eight. They (8) *are / would be / were* all under six when we went and they all had a great time (9) *to admire / admiring / admire* the big rockets. It is only a day trip though, and since our family isn't much into space, we probably (10) *won't go / don't go / wouldn't go* back very soon.
Sam

Score: .... /5

TASK B Change the form of the words in brackets to complete the sentences correctly.

1. All vehicles must be thoroughly .... (EXAM) before entering this area.
2. The effects of those .... (POLLUTE) on the ozone layer are being studied carefully.
3. For one year, he was the only orthopaedic .... (SURGERY) there.
4. Yesterday it was really hot and no matter what I did, I was .... (COMFORT).
5. I've got an .... (APPOINT) with the dentist at three tomorrow.

Score: .... /5

TASK C Complete the conversation with the sentences below. There is one extra sentence.

I have to get going. •
What have you been up to? •
How are you now? • Glad to have you back! •
What about you? • Really, where did you go?

John: Hi Marc, it's been a long time since we last met. (1) ....
Marc: Hi John! It's great to see you again. I've been away on business.
John: (2) ....
Marc: Well, first I flew to London for a couple of days. After that, I flew to Paris, where I had to see some new customers. (3) .... What have you been doing lately?
John: Oh, nothing much. I've been staying at home these past few days. Tina has been away for a week. She's visiting her relatives.
Marc: Well, (4) .... Work is waiting for me. Have a good day.
John: You, too. (5) ....

Score: .... /5

TASK D Complete the text with the phrases below. There are two extra phrases.

to make this happen • because • in addition •
so as to • in particular • while • however

The European Commission works with EU countries (1) .... help them develop their school education systems. (2) .... each country is responsible for the organization and content of its education and training systems, there are advantages in working together on issues of shared concern. (3) ...., the EU adds value by coordinating activities that can help meet common goals and that can provide citizens with greater opportunities for training and study. (4) ...., the EU cooperates with national authorities and education stakeholders to improve policies and exchange good practice. (5) ...., the EU runs a number of funding programmes in the field of education and training.

(*adapted from* http://ec.europa.eu/)

Score: .... /5

Total score: .... /20

83

▶ *INVALSI Trainer*

Language Practice 5

TASK A Underline the right option.

I (1) *was jogging / had jogged / jogged* around my block yesterday when I noticed a blue van with an anonymous logo painted on it. It was just in front of my neighbour's house. I (2) *had not seen / have never seen / never saw* that kind of van in the area. And what's more, I remembered that Ms Johnson had told me she (3) *will be / would be / would have been* away on business (4) *the all / every / the whole* week. In fact, she had asked me to keep an eye on the house for her. I know she's (5) *in collecting / into collecting / for collecting* old books and other antique objects. I immediately thought (6) *I'd better call / I would better call / I'd better to call* the police, (7) *that / which / –* I did on my cell phone. When a man (8) *with / on / in* blue overalls came (9) *out from / out of / from* my neighbour's house carrying a heavy box, a police car was there waiting for him. He (10) *turned up / turned round / turned out* to be a famous art thief.

Score: .... /5

TASK B Change the form of the words in brackets to complete the sentences correctly.

1 The place fell into complete .... (DARK) after sunset.

2 You should introduce more .... (VARY) into your diet.

3 They are celebrating after having .... (SUCCESS) completed their mission.

4 Only a few tickets remain for Sunday afternoon's .... (PERFORM).

5 The .... (ECONOMY) instability is making things worse.

Score: .... /5

TASK C Complete the conversation with the sentences below. There are two extra sentences.

don't mention it. • have you been keeping up? • but it shouldn't be too tough. • what have you been up to? • what's going on? • two more to go? • so you're completely done?

A: Hey Martha. You look tired. (1) ....

B: It's the last week and I have been up all night studying.

A: Ha ha ha. Looks like you are in for a tough week.

B: Tell me about it. How about you? (2) ....

A: I finished all my biology assignments this morning.

B: (3) ....

A: No. I have one more report that is due next Monday. I haven't started it yet, (4) ....

B: How many pages do you have to write?

A: It's a 15-page paper on renewable energy. It's for the physics teacher. By the way, if you need help with your maths assignments, I can help you over the weekend.

B: That would be great. You don't know how much this means to me. Thanks.

A: (5) .... I'll see you on Saturday morning, then. Is that OK for you?

B: Perfect.

Score: .... /5

TASK D Complete the text with the words below. There is one extra word.

whether • because of • that is • despite • both • with the aim to

An International Workshop is taking place in Copenhagen next month (1) .... strengthen existing Water Museums at a global level. (2) .... unprecedented technological progress – or perhaps, rather, (3) .... it – water today is increasingly at risk. Within such a context, the Global Network of Water Museums is an initiative addressed to authorities and citizens who believe in preserving water – (4) .... surface or underground – together with its cultural and historical dimensions. The creation of a Global Network of Water Museums could give a valuable impetus to the emergence of new perspectives concerning water sustainability; (5) .... , paving the way for a paradigm change in water management.

(*adapted from* http://www.unesco.org/

Score: .... /5

Total score: .... /20

84

Language Practice 6

TASK A Underline the right option.

A major search operation (1) *took / takes* place this afternoon after part of a large cliff gave way on a busy beach. (2) *– / The* firefighters and the coastguard scanned the area at Seaford Head, near Eastbourne, East Sussex, despite the fact that (3) *no one / anyone* was reported missing. East Sussex Fire and Rescue Service said it (4) *was called / had been called* to support the coastguard in the search after a cliff (5) *collapsed / has collapsed /* at 4:18 p.m. on Wednesday.
The fire service (6) *sent / has sent* its rescue units to the scene.
East Sussex Fire and Rescue Service said: 'We assisted coastguard to check that no one (7) *caught / was caught* in the fall. All involved worked (8) *hardly / hard*. We'd like to remind the public (9) *stay / to stay* away from cliff edges.' Sean Bradley, duty controller for the UK coastguard, said: 'We (10) *are advising / advised* beach goers to keep away from the scene and we are currently cordoning off the area in the interests of public safety.

Score: .... /5

TASK B Change the form of the words in brackets to complete the sentences correctly.

1 The company has .... (WORLD) connections and a long experience in the field.
2 Temperatures are expected to peak at 34 °C tomorrow and then drop off with the .... (ARRIVE) of thunderstorms.
3 His interest in politics .... (BROAD) as he grew up.
4 Foreigners reveal what they find most .... (ANNOY) about British people.
5 Do you consider yourself a .... (COMPETE) person?

Score: .... /5

TASK C Match the expressions (1-5) with the suitable response (A-E).

☐ 1 Hi! How are things?
☐ 2 Good to see you again.
☐ 3 Hey, it stopped raining! Shall we go out for a walk?
☐ 4 Hi Claire, what have you been up to?
☐ 5 How are you doing?

A Nothing much.
B I'm alright, and you?
C Not too bad, thanks. / Not so good. / So so.
D Pleased to see you too.
E Good call.

Score: .... /5

TASK D Choose TWO expressions from the list that match each situation (1-5).

Definitely! • Good point! • I agree but ... • Up to a point, yes. • I'm not so sure. • How can you possibly say that? • I couldn't agree less! • Fair enough! • You can say that again! • I can't altogether agree.

What do you say to …
1 express strong agreement?
....
2 express agreement with reservations?
....
3 express strong disagreement?
....
4 express weak disagreement?
....
5 concede a point?
....

Score: .... /5

Total score: .... /20

▶ *INVALSI Trainer*

Language Practice 7

B2

TASK A Underline the right option.

Lots of teenage boys have turned (1) *up / out / on* to school wearing skirts after their headteacher (2) *has refused / refused / refuses* to relax the uniform code banning shorts (3) *even if / because of / despite* the high temperatures. Students argued it was too hot for long trousers and asked if they (4) *could have worn / could wear / can wear* shorts. When this (5) *had been refused / refused / was refused* some arrived at school last Wednesday in skirts. On Thursday about 30 boys were wearing skirts.

Score: .... /5

TASK B Change the form of the words in brackets to complete the sentences correctly.

1 Test your German .... (KNOW) with this new puzzle book.
2 The tunnel will be temporarily closed for .... (MAINTAIN).
3 Bicycles these days are so advanced, making cycling an .... (ENJOY) activity.
4 A local primary school will have to share its limited IT .... (EQUIP) after its second burglary in 12 months.
5 The death or .... (LOSE) of a pet can be a traumatic experience.

Score: .... /5

TASK C Choose ONE phrase from the list that matches each situation (1-5). There is one extra phrase.

I haven't a clue. • Nonsense! • Don't forget! • Please don't remember that! • Definitely! • Have you heard that … (Jessica is leaving her job)?

What do you say to …
1 deny? ....
2 ask about knowledge? ....
3 assert ignorance? ....
4 remind someone? ....
5 express confident assertion? ....

Score: .... /5

TASK D This is an interview. Match the questions with the appropriate answer. There are two extra questions.

☐ 1 What do you enjoy the most about environmental health science research?
☐ 2 What do you like to do in your spare time?
☐ 3 Did you know right away that you wanted to be a research scientist?
☐ 4 How did you end up in the field of environmental health science?
☐ 5 How did you become interested in science?
☐ 6 What did you study in graduate school?
☐ 7 What is your advice to students considering a career in science?

(A) ....
As a child I wanted to be a marine biologist. My parents purchased a microscope and telescope for me. I grew up thinking that if I wanted to be a scientist, I could.

(B) ....
I think of environmental health science as the research of environmental science that studies the potential impact on human health. I think I've always done that by studying environmental science from a chemistry standpoint.

(C) ....
The best part is when the science and the people meet. I like it when you have these students and scientists coming together to do something really great, people having fun while they're doing it, people learning while they do it, people respecting each other while they do it.

(D) ....
I think that the first step would be to make contact with someone like me who is a real person and a real scientist and to meet someone like me and see that I'm approachable and not a nerd with big glasses and a pocket protector.

(E) ....
Well, I usually spend time with my two children, surf, bike, hike, and do yoga and Pilates.

(*adapted from* http://unsolvedmysteries.oregonstate.edu/meet_Staci)

Score: .... /5

Total score: .... /20

INVALSI Trainer

Language Practice 8

TASK A Underline the right option.

Disneyland was not the first theme park

When Disneyland (1) *was open / was being opened / was opened*, amusement parks (2) *had been / have been / were* around in the United States for a long time. Disneyland was obviously not the first. (3) *– / The / Some* theme parks, i.e. amusement parks based on one concept, appeared in the US a decade before Disneyland, with Santa Claus Land in Indiana being the originator of the concept in 1946.
What Disneyland offered, (4) *thus / therefore / though*, that differed from its predecessors, was a theme park on a more massive scale. Walt also said at the park opening that 'the idea of Disneyland is a simple one. It will become a place for parents and children to share pleasant times in (5) *their / one another's / the other's* company.'

Score: .... /5

TASK B Change the form of the words in brackets to complete the sentences correctly.

1. Their research has led to a number of important .... (DISCOVER) about the disease.
2. She recorded all her .... (OBSERVE) in a notebook.
3. He suffered from .... (PSYCHOLOGY) disorders all of his life.
4. I heard an .... (ANNOUNCE) saying that the supermarket was closing.
5. All the major newspapers deal with the same topic in their .... (EDITOR) today.

Score: .... /5

TASK C Complete the conversation with the sentences below. There is one extra sentence.

I'm very pleased • something to drink •
are you ready to order, Madam? •
you're welcome • anything else, Madam? •
how do you prefer

Waiter: (1) ....
Customer: Yes, I am. I'll have lasagne and a steak.
Waiter: And (2) .... the steak, Madam?
Customer: Well done, please. And I'd like some mashed potatoes with the steak.
Waiter: OK. Would you like (3) .... ?
Customer: Yes, a glass of red wine, please. Oh, sorry, but could I change the mashed potatoes to some salad, please?
Waiter: Sure. (4) ....
Customer: No, thank you.
Waiter: (5) .... , Madam!

Score: .... /5

TASK D Choose the expression(s) from the list that match each situation (1-3). There is one extra expression.

This is beyond me. • Do you really think so? •
I'm completely baffled. • I'm sure. •
I'm puzzled. • I can't tell you for sure.

What do you say to …

1. express uncertainty?
   ....
2. express doubt?
   ....
3. express bewilderment?
   ....

Score: .... /5

Total score: .... /20

▶ *INVALSI Trainer*

Language Practice 9

B2

TASK A Underline the right option.

The world needs to produce at least 50% more food to feed 9 billion people (1) *by / in / for* 2050. And (2) *if / unless / when* we change how we grow our food and manage our natural capital, food security – especially for the world's poorest – (3) *would be / will be / will have been* at risk. For two decades, leading up to the millennium, global demand for food (4) *will have increased / was increasing / has been increasing* steadily, along with growth (5) *in / of / for* the world's population, record harvests, improvements in incomes, and (6) *– / a / the* diversification of diets. (7) *Since then / However / As a result*, food prices continued to decline (8) *in / till / through* 2000. But beginning in 2004, prices for most grains began (9) *rise / to rising / to rise*. Although there was an increase in production, the increase in demand was (10) *very / extremely / much* greater.

(*adapted from* www.un.org/)

Score: .... /5

TASK B Change the form of the words in brackets to complete the sentences correctly.

1. They suggest reducing our energy .... (CONSUME) and turning to renewable energies.
2. My cousin Pete has always been an .... (AMBITION) person.
3. Will they ever find a .... (SOLVE) to that problem?
4. The hotel services are amazing and beyond .... (COMPARE).
5. This is an example of the kind of .... (ALTERNATE) music going around now.

Score: .... /5

TASK C Complete the conversation with the questions below. There is one extra question.

Can I have a piece of chocolate cake? •
Have you tried a new recipe? •
What are you cooking? •
You don't want to wait until after dinner? •
How was school? • Can I, Mum?

Susie: Mum, I am home.
Mrs Jefferson: (1) ....
Susie: It was OK, and I got a high grade on my biology oral test. Mum, I was so worried about that test, but now I feel fine. What a relief!
Mrs Jefferson: I am glad to hear that. You have been studying so hard the past few weeks.
Susie: (2) ....
It smells so good.
Mrs Jefferson: I am baking cakes. This is your favourite chocolate cake.
Susie: It looks really yummy. And I see biscuits over there too. You were busy, weren't you?
Mrs Jefferson: Yes. Tony has to take something to school tomorrow. So, those biscuits are for him. Don't touch them.
Susie: (3) ....
Mrs Jefferson: (4) ....
Susie: It looks inviting, and I bet it is delicious. No, I don't want to wait. (5) ....
Mrs Jefferson: OK, then, go ahead.

Score: .... /5

TASK D Complete the sentences with ONE of the words below. There is one extra word.

anyway • furthermore • therefore •
consequently • otherwise • on the other hand

1. Nuclear power is cheap. ...., you could argue it's not safe.
2. You'll have to go now, ... you'll miss the bus.
3. The molecules are absorbed into the bloodstream and .... affect the organs.
4. He is old and unpopular. ...., he has at best only two years of political life ahead of him.
5. Progress so far has been very good. We are, ..., confident that the work will be completed on time.

Score: .... /5

Total score: .... /20

Language Practice 10

B2

TASK A Underline the right option.

The future of food and agriculture. Trends and challenges (part I)

Over the past century, enormous progress (1) *have been made / has been made / was made* in improving human welfare worldwide. Societies have changed radically (2) *thanks to / owing to / seeing as* huge leaps in technology, rapid urbanization and innovations in production systems. (3) *Even if / Therefore / Yet* conditions today are still different from the world 'free of fear and want' envisioned (4) *from / by / for* the founders of (5) *– / the / a* United Nations. (6) *In fact, / Because / Whereas* much remains (7) *doing / done / to be done* to fulfil the vision of the Food and Agriculture Organization of the United Nations (FAO), (8) *… so that / which / it* is to create 'a world free of hunger and malnutrition and one in which food and agriculture contribute (9) *to improving / to improve / improving* the living standards of all, especially (10) *the poorer / the surely poorest / the poorest*, in an economically, socially and environmentally sustainable manner'.

(adapted from http://www.fao.org/)

Score: .... /5

TASK B Change the form of the words in brackets to complete the sentences correctly.

The future of food and agriculture. Trends and challenges (part II)

Amid great plenty, billions of people still face pervasive (1) .... (POOR), gross inequalities, joblessness, (2) .... (ENVIRONMENT) degradation, disease and deprivation. Displacement and migratory flows are at their highest levels since the Second World War. While many armed conflicts have been resolved, new ones have emerged. Much of humanity's progress has come at a (3) .... (CONSIDER) cost to the environment. The impacts of climate change are already being felt, and – if left unabated – will intensify considerably in the years ahead. Globally integrated (4) .... (PRODUCE) processes have brought many benefits. However, challenges in regulating those processes highlight the need to steer them towards more equitable and (5) .... (SUSTAIN) outcomes.

(adapted from http://www.fao.org/)

Score: .... /5

TASK C Complete the conversation with the phrases below. There are two extra phrases.

can't miss it! • is it far? • go straight on • excuse me! • a bit complicated • how far is it? • sorry!

A: (1) .... How do I get to the Grand Hotel from here?
B: Ah. It's (2) ....
A: Oh, dear. (3) ....
B: Not really. It'll take about ten minutes on foot. Now, when you leave the roundabout, turn right and after about 500 metres you'll come to the post office. (4) .... another 300 metres till you come to a big square. Opposite the town hall on the main square is the Grand Hotel. You (5) ....
A: Thanks a lot.

Score: .... /5

TASK D Put the paragraphs in the correct order.

UNESCO regrets the UK government's decision to cancel the A303 Stonehenge Road Improvement Scheme …

☐ A urged the State Party of the United Kingdom 'to find an appropriate solution.

☐ B The issue of traffic congestion around Stonehenge has been the subject of discussion at the World Heritage Committee since 2004.

☐ C In its 2005 decision in Durban, South Africa, the Committee regretted that no progress had been made in the implementation of the A303 Stonehenge Improvement Scheme and

☐ D Following the decision to cancel the A303 project, the World Heritage Centre will submit a State of Conservation report to the World Heritage Committee so that it can fully examine the implications of this decision.

☐ E on the basis of cost concerns and hopes that another solution will be found to relieve traffic congestion around the World Heritage property of Stonehenge.

(adapted from http://whc.unesco.org/)

Score: .... /5

Total score: .... /20

▶ INVALSI Trainer

Language Practice 11

B2

TASK A Underline the right option.

A number of factors have played an important role in the evolutionary success of the human species. One of the undeniably fundamental factors (1) *was / have been / has been* our inherent ability to communicate. The project Social Robots is aiming (2) *gain / to gain / gaining* a deeper understanding of the intricacies of how we coordinate our actions with other people and with robots to achieve mutual goals. The project (3) *will be combining / has combined / combined* approaches from disciplines such as Social Cognition, Social Neuroscience and Social Robotics to study populations that vary across age and cultural background. In this way, it (4) *will have provided / will provide / has provided* the most comprehensive picture to date of how a biological system that evolved to support social interactions with other people (5) *will have been adapting / will have adapted / can adapt* to interact with artificial agents.
Over the last decade, smart devices (6) *became / have become / are becoming* a significant part of our lives and the companies that make them (7) *are developing / developed / will develop* new and innovative ways for us to interact with them. In addition, the development of home companion robots and assistance robots for schools and hospitals (8) *has thought to become / is thought to become / thinks of becoming* the norm in just a few years from now.
These artificial agents try to deliver behaviours that (9) *can be considered / can consider / can have considered* 'social' and how we perceive and interact with them remains largely unexplored. They provide social cognition researchers with a brand new opportunity (10) *studying / for the study / to study* how humans respond to different situations during social interaction.

Score: .... /5

TASK B Change the form of the words in brackets to complete the sentences correctly.

1 That girl is so .... (OBEY)! She does everything the first time she is asked.
2 Reaching the top gave him a sense of .... (ACHIEVE).
3 Unfortunately his work is always full of .... (CARE) mistakes.
4 His .... (ABLE) with modern technology caused him to fail the IT exam.
5 Another aspect his teachers blame him for is his constant .... (LAZY).

Score: .... /5

TASK C Match the questions (1-5) with the appropriate answer (A-E).

☐ 1 Which do you prefer, tea or coffee?
☐ 2 How long have you had this scarf?
☐ 3 Do these shoes come in children's sizes?
☐ 4 Whose slippers are those?
☐ 5 Do you think I could ask Paul?

A I don't know. Let me check for you.
B Well, I don't think he can help you.
C I think they're Mike's.
D Neither.
E I've just bought it.

Score: .... /5

TASK D Choose TWO expressions from the list that match each situation (1-5).

I'm looking forward to that. • Oh dear! • Is something worrying you? • Oh!/Ow!/Ouch! • Look after yourself! • What a shame/pity! • You're hurting me! • Take care. • I'm very excited about that! • Is there something on your mind?

What do you say to …

1 express good wishes when parting from someone?
....
2 express regret/sympathy, condolences?
....
3 express hope, expectation?
....
4 enquire about anxiety/worry?
....
5 express pain?
....

Score: .... /5

Total score: .... /20

Language Practice 12

INVALSI Trainer

B2

TASK A Underline the right option.

Since June the European Broadcasting Union (1) *has been / was / is* a partner to a Council of Europe platform designed (2) *to tracking / track / to track* violations of media freedom in member states. The platform (3) *set up / was setting up / was set up* by the Council of Europe to promote the protection of journalism and the safety of journalists.
Council of Europe Secretary General Thorbjørn Jagland (4) *has signed / signed / was signing* the partnership agreement at the EBU's General Assembly where he (5) *has spoken / spoke / speaks* to leading broadcasters on the essential role of public service media in modern democracies.
'I am pleased to welcome the EBU to the platform and I am convinced that this partnership (6) *strengthened / is strengthening / will strengthen* the impact of the Council of Europe in addressing media freedom challenges,' said Jagland at the signature of the Memorandum of Understanding.
The Platform allows partners (7) *issue / issuing / to issue* alerts concerning threats to media freedom. Once the alerts (8) *issue / were issued / are issued*, they are sent to the authorities of the country concerned and to the different Council of Europe institutions. The Council of Europe institutions (9) *may react / would react / react* publicly or start a dialogue on the issue with the authorities. Since April 2015, when the platform (10) *has been launched / launched / was launched*, partner organizations have published 306 alerts.

(adapted from https://rm.coe.int/168072e821)

Score: .... /5

TASK B Change the form of the words in brackets to complete the sentences correctly.

1. Eventually all the .... (BURGLE) were arrested.
2. The lake froze to a .... (DEEP) of over a metre.
3. The accident was followed by two months of pain and .... (BORE) in the hospital.
4. He wanted to become a .... (LAW), just like his father.
5. The police are looking through all the documentary .... (EVIDENT) they have.

Score: .... /5

TASK C Complete the sentences with ONE of the idioms below.

head over heels • saved by the bell •
air your dirty laundry • an arm and a leg •
cut to the chase

1. Don't tell your friends about your brother's problems. You shouldn't ....
2. After a few introductory comments, we .... and the discussion began.
3. It's obvious that Jane and Pete are .... in love with each other.
4. College fees cost .... nowadays.
5. Luckily, the train arrived before I had time to answer her question .... !

Score: .... /5

TASK D Put the paragraphs in the correct order to read the complete synopsis of the book 'Stay: a Girl, a Dog, a Bucket List'.

Eli the dog has been with Astrid since her parents brought her home from the hospital as a baby.

☐ A But in the end, what is most important to Eli is the time he spends with Astrid, whom he loves dearly.

☐ B Now Astrid is getting older, and so is Eli.

☐ C So she makes a bucket list for Eli, which includes experiences such as eating with him in a restaurant, and taking him down a slide at the playground.

☐ D The authors have created a story that reminds readers of all ages that time with our loved ones is the most precious gift of all.

☐ E Before he slows down too much, Astrid wants to make fun memories with him.

Score: .... /5

Total score: .... /20

▶ INVALSI Trainer

Language Practice 13

B2

TASK A Underline the right option.

I love (1) *discover / to discovering / discovering* a new place completely by chance. I (2) *had done / had made / had taken* a lot of research on Sicily beforehand, but one of my favourite places turned (3) *up / on / out* to be a little seaside town I (4) *haven't even heard of / didn't even hear of / hadn't even heard of* until the day my mum, my best friend, and I (5) *visited / were visiting / had visited* it.
It was our second morning in Sicily and we (6) *didn't feel / hadn't felt / weren't feeling* too energetic, but we wanted to get out and see (7) *anything / something / everything*.
'Why don't you go to Aci Trezza?' our host Anna suggested.
Hmm. I hadn't heard of that. My mum and Maria started discussing the town as I absentmindedly scrolled (8) *from / through / over* Snapchat, overhearing snippets of their speech every now and again.
Half an hour later, without knowing (9) *everything /something / anything* beyond Anna's testimonial, we (10) *set off for / sent out for / sailed on to* Aci Trezza.

Score: .... /5

TASK B Change the form of the words in brackets to complete the sentences correctly.

1 In my own experience, most web users are still .... (AWARE) of its assets.
2 A shorter jacket would better emphasize her .... (HIGH).
3 He was given an .... (INJECT) of local anaesthetic.
4 We are all constantly exposed to .... (POISON) chemicals or toxins.
5 I missed his webinar on Tuesday but .... (LUCK) it has been rescheduled for tomorrow.

Score: .... /5

TASK C Choose ONE expression from the list that matches each situation (1-5). There are two extra expressions

It was the least I could do.
• Fancy a drink? • Would you like any help? •
I really can't thank you enough! •
OK, I'll help you! •
Congratulations! You really deserved that. •
It's very good of you!

What do you say …
1 to help an old person to carry a heavy bag?
....
2 to come to the end of your stay with a family in a foreign country?
....
3 when your classmate asks for help with his homework?
....
4 to invite a friend out?
....
5 to meet a person who has just won the first prize in a sports event?
....

Score: .... /5

TASK D Complete the text with the words below. There are two extra words.

so • later • but • like • instead of • as • before

I started practising and filming extreme sports when I saw a snowboard for the very first time (1) .... a teenager. I was totally attracted by this brand new sport and one year (2) .... I got my first snowboard. Just about the same time I started to get into photography. So it was just a question of time to combine both my passions, snowboarding and photography. I even started studying medicine. (3) .... after a while I found out that my passion was extreme sports and storytelling. I wanted to let other people take part in the sensations I had. (4) .... in 1999 I started videography. It was a new challenge to show extreme sports in moving (5) .... still pictures.

Score: .... /5

Total score: .... /20

Language Practice 14

B2

TASK A Underline the right option.

Hokey Pokey

(1) *The / A / –* Blogger Monica Jefferson features recipes, photos, and distant places on her blog 'Hokey Pokey'. She (2) *had moved / moved / was moving* to New York 12 years ago from New Zealand and works (3) *in / for / with* the legal industry alongside her blogging career. (4) *As / Like / How* a freelance recipe developer and writer, Monica (5) *was spoken / has spoken / is speaking* at blogging conferences, covering topics from (6) *– / a / the* legal aspects of blogging to recipe writing and editing. Monica (7) *feels / is feeling / was feeling* that the story of what she likes to cook is the story of her life and that (8) *the food and travel / the food and the travel / food and travel* are the two things that she has been in love with (9) *for / when / since* childhood. 'Hokey Pokey' gets (10) *their / her / its* name from a creamy vanilla ice cream with pieces of honeycomb which is very common in New Zealand.

Score: .... /5

TASK B Change the form of the words in brackets to complete the sentences correctly.

1 When she put on all those old clothes we thought she looked .... (RIDICULE).
2 He said that it was a matter of national .... (SECURE).
3 What could I use to .... (SWEET) the taste?
4 The shop was .... (THOROUGH) cleaned to make a fresh new start.
5 The old building is being returned to its .... (ORIGIN) style.

Score: .... /5

TASK C Replace the underlined word or phrase with ONE of the idioms below. There is one extra idiom.

on the tip of his tongue • getting my feet wet • busy as a bee • blue • keep a straight face • getting on my nerves

1 My sister has been really <u>sad</u> since her dog died last week.
   Idiom: ....
2 James had the answer <u>ready</u>, but Matt said it first.
   Idiom: ....
3 It was hard to <u>look serious and not laugh</u> when Sue imitated the history teacher.
   Idiom: ....
4 I'm just <u>getting ready</u>, so I'd like some tips about the final exam.
   Idiom: ....
5 All this noise is <u>annoying me a lot</u>.
   Idiom: ....

Score: .... /5

TASK D Choose the expression(s) from the list that match each situation (1-6).

Cross fingers! • If you must. • Many happy returns! • It's very kind of you but I can't. • Please do! • Well done! • By all means! • Brilliant! • I'm afraid I can't. • I can't stop you, can I?

What do you say to …
1 grant permission?
   ....
2 grant permission with reluctance?
   ....
3 decline an offer or invitation?
   ....
4 congratulate someone?
   ....
5 express good wishes on someone's birthday?
   ....
6 wish someone success?
   ....

Score: .... /5

Total score: .... /20

▶ INVALSI Trainer

Language Practice 15

B2

TASK A Underline the right option.

Over (1) *–* / *the* / *those* last two weeks, residents of Wales have reported (2) *seeing* / *to see* / *see* a strange shimmering object in the sky (3) *it* / *–* / *which* is believed (4) *being* / *been* / *to be* proof that extraterrestrials (5) *will visit* / *visited* / *are visiting*.
The odd phenomenon (6) *is first spotted* / *first spotted* / *was first spotted* on Sunday by a surfer who caught it (7) *on* / *in* / *to* his camera. And after he (8) *has been posting* / *has posted* / *posted* the video on Facebook, it went viral. Since then, a flurry of videos (9) *have been uploaded* / *are uploaded* / *were uploaded* to social media sites, all of which (10) *are made* / *are making* / *have been made* in different locations across Wales.

Score: .... /5

TASK B Change the form of the words in brackets to complete the sentences correctly.

The European Central Bank (ECB) is an official institution of the European Union that is located in Frankfurt am Main, Germany. Its two key (1) .... (RESPONSIBLE) are monetary policy for the countries which have adopted the euro and European banking supervision (all euro area countries participate (2) .... (AUTOMATIC) in the system of banking supervision while other EU countries that do not yet have the euro as their currency can choose to participate).
The staff of the ECB, who come from across the European Union, work (3) .... (CLOSE) with the national central banks in the euro area to deliver and maintain price (4) .... (STABLE) – the value of our money – as well as with the national supervisory authorities to ensure sound banking supervision. Our common currency, the euro, has drawn almost 340 million European citizens closer together and is a strong symbol of unity in (5) .... (DIVERSE).

(*adapted from* http://ec.europa.eu/)

Score: .... /5

TASK C Match the first part of the sentence (1-5) with the second part (A-E).

☐ 1 Would you mind ...
☐ 2 I'll pencil you in ...
☐ 3 **A**: Mr Grey, you have a call from Ms Jackson. **B**: ...
☐ 4 Thanks for ...
☐ 5 Good morning. This is Charlotte. ...

A for 9 on Thursday.
B holding for a second?
C How can I help you?
D calling. Take care.
E Great! Put her through.

Score: .... /5

TASK D Complete the text with the words below. There are two extra words.

finally • in turn • however • meanwhile • after • where • unfortunately

Marie Curie (1867-1934) was a famous Polish scientist. She studied at Sorbonne University in Paris, (1) .... in 1893 she gained a degree in physics. A year later she gained a degree in maths. In 1894 she met Pierre Curie. They got married in 1895. (2) .... a German named Wilhelm Röntgen discovered X-rays. Then in 1896 Antoine Henri Becquerel discovered that uranium gives off mysterious, invisible rays. In 1897 Marie Curie started investigating uranium. In 1898 she coined the term 'radioactive' to describe any substance that gave off the mysterious rays. Marie also examined a substance called 'pitchblende', which she realized must contain some elements that are much more radioactive than pure uranium. In 1898 Marie and her husband Pierre isolated an element they called 'polonium' (after Poland). (3) .... , they realized there was another element in pitchblende. (4) .... , in 1902 they isolated radium. In 1903 Marie and Pierre Curie were awarded the Nobel Prize for Physics along with Henri Becquerel. (5) .... , Pierre and Marie Curie did not realize that exposure to radiation was harming their health. Marie Curie died on 4th July 1934. She was 66 years old.

Score: .... /5

Total score: .... /20

94

SIMULAZIONE DI PROVA NAZIONALE

Dopo esserti allenato con i task delle pagine precedenti, sei pronto ad affrontare la simulazione di una prova INVALSI completa che ha tutte le caratteristiche della prova che dovrai affrontare nella seconda parte del quinto anno scolastico.

La prova INVALSI per l'ascolto si compone di cinque task: due per il livello B1 e tre per il livello B2. A ogni task corrisponde un **file audio di massimo 4 minuti** e il numero totale di quesiti della prova sarà di 35/40. Il file audio potrebbe essere un monologo o un dialogo tra due o massimo tre persone, oppure una sequenza di piccoli monologhi di circa 20 secondi con speaker e accenti diversi. Prima di iniziare con l'ascolto del file audio avrai a disposizione un minuto per leggere le domande, mentre al termine del secondo ascolto avrai un altro minuto.

Per quanto concerne la lettura, **la prova INVALSI per la lettura si compone di cinque task**: due di livello B1 e tre di livello B2. Il numero totale dei quesiti sarà di 35/40 e la lunghezza massima del testo da leggere e comprendere sarà di **350 parole per il testo del livello B1 e 600 per il testo B2**.

Leggi bene le istruzioni e buona fortuna!

▶ *Listening Comprehension 1*

Lanzarote is Riding the Wave

TASK Multiple Choice Questions

B1

🎧 **26** Listen to what Sergio Rodman, owner of a trendy surfing school, says about Lanzarote.

First you will have 1 minute to study the task below, then you will hear the recording twice. While listening, choose the correct answer (A, B, C or D) for questions 1-7.
Only one answer is correct.
The first one (0) has been done for you.

After the second listening, you will have 1 minute to check your answers.

0   What links architect César Manrique to Lanzarote?
☐ A   His House Museum opened last year and soon became a tourist attraction.
☐ B   He was born in Lanzarote.
☐ C   He transformed the island into an open-air museum.
☒ D   *He had a major impact on the island.*

1   Which is the best time of year to visit the island for skilled surfers?
☐ A   Spring.
☐ B   Summer.
☐ C   Autumn.
☐ D   Winter.

2   Why does Sergio Rodman suggest having a surf instructor on your first days in Lanzarote?
☐ A   Mainly for safety reasons.
☐ B   It is a fast way to learn the tricks.
☐ C   An instructor can tell you where the best spots are.
☐ D   Because you can't surf alone in some spots.

3   What's special about Camino de Los Gracioseros according to Sergio Rodman?
☐ A   It is suitable for beginners, too.
☐ B   It offers wonderful views.
☐ C   It runs along some of the best beaches.
☐ D   It is not very long.

4   What special feature of Casa Luis does Sergio Rodman seem to appreciate?
☐ A   The friendly staff.
☐ B   Live music.
☐ C   You eat sitting on the rocks.
☐ D   The low budget prices.

5   What special food is served at Casa Luis?
☐ A   Very traditional dishes.
☐ B   Only organic food.
☐ C   Fresh fish.
☐ D   Local produce only.

6   What kind of beaches are to be found in the Calas de Papagayo?
☐ A   Sandy.
☐ B   Pebbly.
☐ C   Wide.
☐ D   Volcanic.

7   What can you have at Chiringuito?
☐ A   Only fish dishes.
☐ B   Grilled meat.
☐ C   A special cocktail.
☐ D   Paella with dark rice.

Score: .... /7

Listening Comprehension 2

Uffizi Records

TASK Short Answer Questions

B1

🎧 27 Listen to the records the Uffizi Gallery in Florence has recently set.

First you will have 1 minute to study the task below, then you will hear the recording twice.
While listening, answer the questions (1-8) using a maximum of 4 words.
Write your answers in the spaces provided.
The first one (0) has been done for you.

After the second listening, you will have 1 minute to check your answers.

0	How many tickets were sold last year?	*Over 4 / four million.*
1	How much more did the Uffizi earn last year?	
2	What contributed to set such a record?	
3	What is the position of the Uffizi Gallery in the social media national ranking?	
4	How does the Uffizi Gallery rank on social media worldwide?	
5	What is the Uffizi's most popular work of art on social media?	
6	On which social media platforms does the Uffizi Gallery have a profile?	
7	How long has the Uffizi Gallery had its own website?	
8	Which social media platform has a lot of followers from abroad?	

Score: .... /8

▶ *Listening Comprehension 3*

LA LA Land Reloaded

TASK Multiple Choice Questions

B2

🎧 **28** Listen to a description of modern Los Angeles.

First you will have 1 minute to study the task below, then you will hear the recording twice. While listening, choose the correct answer (A, B, C or D) for questions 1-8.
Only one answer is correct.
The first one (0) has been done for you.

After the second listening, you will have 1 minute to check your answers.

0 What kind of image of Los Angeles did Ridley Scott give in his 1982 film?
- [ ] A A better place than it actually is now.
- [ ] B An abandoned place with a gloomy future.
- [ ] C A town inhabited by aliens.
- [X] **D A megacity with lots of problems.**

1 What's Los Angeles really like now?
- [ ] A A relaxed place with a vibrant cultural life.
- [ ] B A worse place than in the film.
- [ ] C A modern city with some traditional aspects.
- [ ] D The same as in Ridley Scott's film.

2 Which is LA's most attractive area now?
- [ ] A The area around Hollywood.
- [ ] B The city centre.
- [ ] C The coastal area.
- [ ] D The commercial district.

3 What happened to DTLA between 1950 and the end of the last century?
- [ ] A Modern hotels replaced old historic buildings.
- [ ] B Wealthy people abandoned DTLA.
- [ ] C Important companies moved their headquarters there.
- [ ] D Huge investments were made to improve the area.

4 What is Skid Row known for?
- [ ] A Vagabonds and poor people still live on the street.
- [ ] B Young artists set up their studios there.
- [ ] C Fashionable restaurants have recently been opened there.
- [ ] D Modern skyscrapers are everywhere.

5 What kind of city does author Dorothy Parker refer to?
- [ ] A A sprawling city.
- [ ] B A multicultural city.
- [ ] C A fragmented city.
- [ ] D A city with no identity.

6 What is special about LA's Broadway today?
- [ ] A The elegant buildings once used as cinemas are still there.
- [ ] B Modern multiplex cinemas are located in Art Deco buildings.
- [ ] C More and more luxury boutiques are being opened.
- [ ] D Production companies are moving their studios there.

7 Where in DTLA does a walking tour of the set of 'Blade Runner' start from?
- [ ] A From the Mexican area.
- [ ] B From Grand Central Market.
- [ ] C From the Bradbury Building.
- [ ] D From LA Union Station.

8 Where can you go to spend some time on the beach in LA?
- [ ] A To the west of LA.
- [ ] B To K-Town.
- [ ] C To the south of LA.
- [ ] D To Silver Lake.

Score: ………. /8

Listening Comprehension 4

Nicole Kidman

TASK Multiple Matching (Matching interview)

B2

🎧 29 Listen to an interview with Nicole Kidman.

First you will have 1 minute to study the task below, then you will hear the recording twice.
While listening, match the interviewer's questions (A-K) with the answers (1-8).
There are two extra questions that you do not need to use.
The first one (0) has been done for you.

After the second listening, you will have 1 minute to check your answers.

	Questions	Answers	
A	Is it true that you and your husband never text?	0	E
B	Was turning 50 a problem?	1	
C	In one of your movies you play a criminal. Have your ever been in trouble with the law?	2	
D	Were you a rebel when you were young?	3	
E	*How do you find the time to be a parent when you make so many movies?*	4	
F	Do you understand your mother now that you have four kids?	5	
G	Is raising children hard work?	6	
H	What is the best decision you have ever made?	7	
I	Do you consider yourself a vain person?	8	
J	Is having a supportive family important for your career?		
K	How do people react to you and your family?		

Score: .... /8

▶ *Listening Comprehension 5*

The Future of Food
TASK Multiple Matching (Matching sentences)

🎧 30 Listen to an expert talking about the future of food.

First you will have 1 minute to study the task below, then you will hear the recording twice. While listening, match the beginnings of the sentences (1-8) with the sentence endings (A-K). There are two sentence endings that you do not need to use.
The first one (0) has been done for you.

After the second listening, you will have 1 minute to check your answers.

0	Dr Lind proved that ...	F
1	In 2015 it was found that ...	
2	DNA testing can ...	
3	Most of the vegetables we eat today are ...	
4	Our current produce has ...	
5	Thanks to advanced DNA technology ...	
6	A special molecule has led to ...	
7	All senses play a role in the way ...	
8	The findings of 'neurogastronomy' will ...	

A	unlock personalized nutrition.
B	genetically modified crop varieties will increase.
C	be applied to the restaurant of the future.
D	the creation of a meat-free burger.
E	variations in our organs' internal physiology.
F̶	*our health conditions depend on our diet.*
G	give delayed bursts of flavour in the mouth.
H	the result of selective breeding.
I	we may react differently to the same foods.
J	fewer nutrients and minerals than in the past.
K	we react to how food tastes in our mouths.

Score: .... /8

100

The International Labour Organization

TASK Multiple Choice Questions

Read the text about the International Labour Organization (ILO), then choose the correct answer (A, B, C or D) for questions 1-7.

The first one (0) has been done for you.

The International Labour Organization (ILO) is a UN agency which brings together governments, employers and workers of 187 Member States, to promote rights at work, encourage decent employment opportunities, enhance social protection and strengthen dialogue on work-related issues.

It was founded in 1919, at the end of a destructive war, to pursue a vision based on the idea that peace can be established only if it is based on social justice. The ILO, which became the first specialized agency of the UN in 1946, has played an influential role in key historical moments, including the Great Depression, decolonization and the end of apartheid in South Africa. In 1969, on its 50th anniversary, the ILO was awarded the Nobel Prize for Peace.

Its structure is unique and is based on the rule that representatives of governments, workers and employers are all equal in the decision-making process. The ILO's Secretariat has its headquarters in Geneva, Switzerland, and a global network of technical experts and field offices in more than 40 countries. Every year the Member States of the ILO meet at the International Labour Conference in June. Employer and worker delegates can freely express

► *Reading Comprehension 1*

themselves and vote according to
the instructions of their organizations.
They sometimes vote against
each other or even against their
35 government representatives.
The Conference establishes and
adopts international labour standards.
It also votes the Organization's
budget and elects the Governing
40 Body, which is the executive council
of the ILO and meets three times
a year in Geneva.

Its field of action includes wages,
pensions, discrimination, freedom
45 of association, the rights of children,
domestic workers and seafarers.
The ILO is not only about better
working conditions for individuals.
Its aims include the creation of
50 a fairer society.

The ILO's contribution was essential
when Agenda 2030 for Sustainable
Development chose to place decent
work for all at the heart of policies
55 for sustainable and inclusive growth
and development.

0 **The International Labour Organization (ILO) is an independent agency of …**
☐ A the European Union.
☒ B the United Nations.
☐ C UNICEF.
☐ D NATO.

1 **The current number of countries represented at the ILO is …**
☐ A 40.
☐ B 169.
☐ C 187.
☐ D 50.

2 **The ILO was originally established …**
☐ A during a peace conference.
☐ B in 1919.
☐ C independently of the UN.
☐ D as a trade union.

3 **It received the Nobel Prize for Peace …**
☐ A in 1919.
☐ B in 1950.
☐ C in 1946.
☐ D in 1969.

Reading Comprehension 1

4 The ILO's main offices are …
☐ A in more than 40 countries.
☐ B in Switzerland.
☐ C in different places around the world.
☐ D at the UN headquarters.

5 At the ILO Conference the right to vote belongs to the representatives of …
☐ A Member States, workers, and employers.
☐ B workers and employers.
☐ C Member States only.
☐ D the Governing Body.

6 The ILO sets standards for …
☐ A disabled workers.
☐ B human rights.
☐ C the elimination of forced labour.
☐ D all of the above.

7 The ILO's main aim is …
☐ A the promotion of rights at work.
☐ B the fight against all forms of discrimination.
☐ C providing training services to worker organizations.
☐ D sustainable development.

Score: ………. /7

▶ Reading Comprehension 2

Wimbledon Whites Just Go Green

TASK Multiple Matching (Gap-fill)

B1

Read the text about how the Wimbledon tennis tournament is embracing sustainability.
Parts of the text have been removed.
Choose the correct part (A-K) for each gap (1-8).
There are two extra parts that you do not need to use.

The first one (0) has been done for you.

The all-white dress code is a rule at Wimbledon, but this year some players are (0) __C__ . Current champion Angelique
5 Kerber, 2017 winner Garbiñe Muguruza and former world No 1 Caroline Wozniacki are among the stars (1) .... designed by Stella McCartney. The outfits were created using material
10 made from plastic waste – and with (2) ....
This is the first time McCartney has created (3) .... for a Grand Slam. Some top men's players, including
15 Stefanos Tsitsipas and Alexander Zverev will also wear the new Adidas collection, which used methods such as 'Dope Dye Technology', which creates (4) .... as materials are dyed at an early stage of
20 production.
During the presentation of the new collection the tennis stars said it was important that athletes did their part for the planet – and urged fans
25 and fellow athletes (5) ....
Spanish star Muguruza said:
'I love being outside. I believe that the better the environment is around us, the better we
30 feel.' Austrian former world No 4 Thiem added: 'Environmental issues are a huge problem in our time, and it's very important that athletes and big companies take steps
35 to (6) .... for future generations to come.' Rising German star Zverev said: 'We train outdoors, we do everything outdoors, so it's important to protect those spaces for future generations.'

40 Last year, Wimbledon bosses banned plastic straws at the All England Club. Plastic bags will also be removed from the player racket-stringing operation, meaning there will be about 4,500 fewer
45 bags used on site. More staff have been hired this year to (7) .... In a press-conference last Tuesday the Wimbledon chief executive, Richard Lewis, said there would also be (8) .... for public
50 use in the grounds, as well as 21 water fountains. The number of water points had nearly doubled since 2014, he added.

104

Reading Comprehension 2

A	a synthetic fibre made from bottles and old clothes
B	87 free water refill points available
C	*going decidedly green*
D	take care of the planet
E	minimize fossil fuel use as much as possible
F	to do the same
G	less water waste
H	help spectators recycle bottles and food packaging
I	wearing a new environmentally-friendly sportswear collection
J	a water recycling plant
K	both women's and men's kit

Score: .... /8

▶ *Reading Comprehension 3*

Hotels in Dublin

TASK Multiple Matching (Matching short texts)

B2

Read the reviews of different hotels in Dublin, then choose the correct texts (A-F) to answer the questions (1-8).
You can use a text more than once.
Write your answers in the spaces provided.

The first one (0) has been done for you.

A Grafton Hotel

This ultra-modern 4-star hotel comes with a bamboo shaded courtyard, legendary gourmet food prepared every day with fresh local ingredients and a chic cocktail bar. Situated in the cultural heart of the city, the Grafton Hotel prides itself on innovative design. It combines both design and style in its creatively designed rooms. All of the guest rooms make use of both space and light and showcase contemporary art and designer furniture complete with rainfall shower bathrooms. A great choice for an ultra-central hotel!

B Miller Hotel

A top luxury hotel in Dublin, the 5-star exceptionally rated Miller Hotel is located in the city centre. The rooms at this trendy Dublin accommodation feature a blend of contemporary and traditional furnishings in keeping with its beautiful Victorian façade. The spacious rooms all have sumptuous beds with top quality linens, free Wi-Fi, flat-screen TVs and iPods loaded with city walking tours. Other hotel highlights include a fitness room, an ornate Irish restaurant and a hip cocktail bar – a perfect place to treat yourself or a loved one!

C Trinity City Hotel

This Dublin hotel offers a luxurious oasis in the very heart of the city just opposite the historic Trinity College. The 4-star very highly regarded Trinity City Hotel prides itself on its modern chic versus magical vintage feel, and its impeccable and striking design. This combination of the old and the new is to be found in the hotel's restaurant, too. The front lounge has panoramic views over Pearse Street, the attractive courtyard garden is an oasis in the middle of the city, perfect for a romantic *al fresco* meal, and the piano lounge is a great place for a relaxed lunch with colleagues. Easily one of the trendiest and most interesting hotels in Dublin!

D Dylan Hotel

Located only 2 km away from the heart of the Irish capital, rooms at the 4-star Dylan Hotel come with all the cool stuff a hipster could wish for – Irish modern art, amps to connect your devices to, Netflix, a Nespresso machine and a heap of designer goods to keep you clean, comfortable and rested. The onsite Bar Bistro takes its inspiration from local culture and stories and uses only the best fresh, homegrown ingredients. With its summer terrace and regular live music, Dylan Hotel is a very popular spot for all generations of guests.

E | Number 61

With its river-facing rooms, Number 61 is one of the most beloved hotels in Dublin City Centre and always seems to top many a review list. The rooms at this quirky Dublin boutique have a cool classy 60's feel. Guests can relax in the leafy courtyard and secluded garden and fortify themselves with what is said to be 'the best breakfast in Dublin' – all organic of course! All of this is further perfected by the old-style Irish charm and hospitality of the staff! A gorgeous and unique Dublin accommodation option.

F | Genesis Hostel

If you would rather save your money for exploring the city, then Genesis Hostel could be the place for you – especially if you're a hipster on a tight budget! Situated in the hip Smithfield District of Dublin next to the Jameson Distillery, this is a cool place. With plenty of innovative communal spaces and a room choice for every budget, this is an ideal place to stay if you are travelling alone and want to meet people. It also offers a luxury hot tub room and clean comfortable shared rooms for small groups and couples, too. Be sure to sample a whiskey in the super Jameson inspired bar!

Which hotel would you choose if you … ?

0	like the idea of starting your day with a healthy meal	E
1	don't intend to spend much on accommodation	
2	are looking for the perfect combination of modernity and vintage	
3	want to stay near the Liffey River	
4	prefer a stylish place not far from museums and theatres	
5	want to enjoy traditional food outside while listening to a band playing live music	
6	want to taste refined, elaborate dishes prepared with local produce	
7	prefer staying in one of the most exclusive hotels in Dublin	
8	invite someone to a business meal	

Score: ………. /8

Reading Comprehension 4

Bicycle Kingdom

TASK Multiple Choice Questions

B2

Read the text about how China is using cycling as a way to fight air pollution, then choose the correct answer (A, B, C or D) for questions 1-8.

The first one (0) has been done for you.

'Bicycle Kingdom' makes a comeback, as China seeks solutions to tackle air pollution crisis

Until the late 1990s, China was a nation of cyclists. Then, from 1995 to 2002, the government created bicycle-reduction policies in
5 order to encourage the growth of the car industry and usage of the mass transit infrastructure. Today, local authorities struggling with traffic and high levels of air pollution have been
10 trying to put residents back on two wheels.

In Hangzhou, a city in eastern China that Marco Polo once described as 'the finest and most
15 splendid city in the world,' air pollution has had a devastating effect with levels well over the safe limit set by the World Health Organization (WHO). In an effort
20 to improve public health and the environment, the Hangzhou authorities have put a great emphasis on cycling, which is helping to cut pollution. Over the
25 past decade, the local government has been improving bike-friendly infrastructure, such as lanes and traffic signals created solely for cyclists, and has provided almost
30 86,000 public bikes. A smart card allows users to easily access all forms of public transport, from bikes to boats to buses.

'All together there have been
35 760 million rides; that's almost half the population of China,' says Tao Xuejun, general manager of the Hangzhou Public Bicycle Service. 'Other cities have followed our
40 example. So far, more than 400 cities in China have adopted our project. Our dream is to promote our model across China and all over the world.'

45 As a result of these initiatives, cycling has become a popular choice for both local citizens and tourists, with important international recognition, too.

50 As well as leading the Chinese cycling resurgence, Hangzhou is home to an innovative way to encourage more sustainable lifestyles, with an app that is
55 helping to stop desertification, cut air pollution and plant millions of new trees. The 'Ant Forest' mini-program incites users to make small, environmentally friendly
60 decisions in their daily lives, such as cycling rather than driving to work, or recycling clothes. When users perform any carbon-reducing activities, they are rewarded with
65 'green energy' points. When they accumulate enough virtual points, a real tree is planted. According to authorities, more than 100 million trees have been planted, thanks
70 to the low-carbon actions of 500 million individuals, roughly 5% of the world's population.

Internationally, one of the best-known examples of harmful air
75 pollution with a negative impact on quality of life is the Chinese capital, Beijing. The causes of Beijing's widespread air pollution can be attributed to a number of factors:
80 an enormous economic boom, a surge in the number of motorized vehicles, population growth, and output from manufacturing.

Fine particulates – tiny, invisible
85 airborne particles – are largely responsible for deaths and illnesses caused by air pollution. The smallest, and deadliest, are called PM 2.5 particles, which bypass the body's
90 defences and lodge in the lungs, bloodstream and brain. Today, fine particulate pollution in Beijing's air is 7.3 times WHO's annual safe level, but local and regional governments
95 have managed to improve the situation in recent years. By using legal, economic and technological tools, the concentration of fine particles in the air has fallen
100 by one third.

'Beijing has achieved impressive air quality improvements in a short amount of time,' said Dechen Tsering, Director of UN Environment's Asia
105 Pacific Regional Office. China's capital city is often cited as a good example of how a large city can balance environmental protection and economic growth, which is one
110 of the challenges many other cities around the world are facing.

(adapted from https://news.un.org/en/story/2019/06/1039751)

Reading Comprehension 4

0 Why was China called the 'Bicycle Kingdom'?
- [ ] A Because of its important cycling policies.
- [X] *B Because cycling used to be very popular.*
- [ ] C Because it invested a lot in bike-friendly infrastructure.
- [ ] D Because of the high quantity of bikes once manufactured.

1 What happened in China between 1995 and 2002?
- [ ] A Lots of people were employed by car factories.
- [ ] B National authorities encouraged a massive use of the bike.
- [ ] C Motor vehicles became the primary private means of transport.
- [ ] D Lots of public funds were spent to improve public transport.

2 What is leading Chinese authorities to encourage a return to cycling?
- [ ] A Serious pollution and congestion issues.
- [ ] B China's car density.
- [ ] C The rising cost of fuel.
- [ ] D Stronger commitment to environmental protection.

3 What has been done in Hangzhou to encourage people to leave their cars at home?
- [ ] A Low-cost electric bicycles have been made available to everyone.
- [ ] B The city provides innovative rental services.
- [ ] C Petrol-powered vehicles have been banned from the centre.
- [ ] D The city has added more bike lanes, more public bikes, and the SIM you use for bike hire also works on other means of transport.

4 Where else has Hangzhou's innovative bicycle scheme been adopted?
- [ ] A In China's capital city.
- [ ] B All over the world.
- [ ] C Nowhere else so far.
- [ ] D In many other Chinese cities.

5 In the Ant Forest scheme, when is a real tree planted in the desert?
- [ ] A After a user has accumulated enough 'green energy' points by doing low-carbon activities.
- [ ] B Any time a person performs low-carbon activities.
- [ ] C As soon as the app is downloaded.
- [ ] D Any time a user gets at least one 'green energy' point.

6 How many people have contributed to the Ant Forest Scheme so far?
- [ ] A More than one hundred million.
- [ ] B Five hundred million.
- [ ] C Fifteen hundred million.
- [ ] D Five thousand million.

7 Which of the following is mentioned as a possible cause of air pollution in Beijing?
- [ ] A Natural phenomena.
- [ ] B Seasonal weather changes.
- [ ] C A dramatic rise in wealth.
- [ ] D Major economic growth.

8 What makes PM 2.5 particles extremely dangerous?
- [ ] A Their invisibility.
- [ ] B They can worsen chronic diseases.
- [ ] C The fact they can get deep into lungs.
- [ ] D Their method of transmission.

Score: .... /8

▶ Reading Comprehension 5

Women Say No to High Heels at Work

TASK Short Answer Questions

B2

Read the article about women's dress code at work in Japan, then complete the sentences (1-8) using a maximum of 4 words.
Write your answers in the spaces provided.

The first one (0) has been done for you.

Thousands of women join campaign to ban workplace high heel requirements

We're used to talking about high heels in terms of fashion, fantasy and even feminism. But we're somewhat less accustomed to speaking about them as business etiquette and workplace obligation – even though, to many women, that's exactly what they represent. High heels have long been seen as a female equivalent to the businessman's necktie. They're an accessory that, when worn in a business setting, send a message of formality and professionalism. Nowhere has this been more true than in the highly gendered corporate culture of Japan where, for years, many companies have required women to wear high heels at work. Recently the practice has been called into question and more than 20 thousand people in Japan have signed a petition to ban the requirement.

The petition was started by Tokyo artist, writer and feminist Yumi Ishikawa. Last January she tweeted about her frustration over being required to wear 2-inch heels for her part-time job as a receptionist at a funeral parlor. 'I like my job right now but wearing pumps is really so hard,' one of her tweets said. 'Of course, if you want to wear them, please go ahead.' Her tweets gained over 67,000 likes and almost 30,000 retweets.

Ishikawa coined the hashtag #KuToo in her tweets, which is a play on two Japanese words – kutsu, meaning 'shoes', and kutsuu, meaning 'pain'. #KuToo has since been used by women to talk about their experiences on social media. At last count, the petition had collected more than 23,000 signatures. Campaigners say wearing high heels in Japan is near-obligatory when job hunting or working in many Japanese companies. Some campaigners describe high heels as akin to modern-day foot-binding, while others have urged a broader loosening of dress codes in Japan.

When asked about the petition, Takumi Nemoto, Japan's health and labour minister, appeared to defend heels-on-the-job. 'It is socially accepted as something that falls within the realm of being occupationally necessary and appropriate,' he said. Employees' health and safety need to be protected, said Nemoto, who oversees the country's workplace reforms. He added there were no plans to change the laws around whether employers could require staff to wear certain clothes or shoes. He noted that men were also subject to rules, as they were often required to wear ties and leather shoes.

In recent years, campaigns such as #KuToo have brought Japan's gender inequality problems into the spotlight. Japan is ranked at 110 out of 149 countries in the World Economic Forum's index measuring the degree of gender equality. Countries around the world have also been cracking down on workplace dress codes in recent years. In Britain, a huge professional services firm became the target of ridicule after receptionist Nicola Thorp was sent home without pay for not wearing the required 5- to 10-cm-high heels in December 2015. Dissatisfied, Thorp began an online petition that garnered over 150,000 signatures, subsequently triggering a debate in Parliament. Although the British government concluded the existing law was adequate in banning gender-based discrimination, it published guidelines in May 2018 titled 'Dress codes and sex discrimination – what you need to know' outlining how the law could be applied in the workplace.

At the 2016 Cannes Film Festival in France, Julia Roberts and many other actresses stunned photographers when they walked the red carpet barefoot or in sneakers to cast light on the event's dress code. Their protest came after a number of women were barred from entering a screening for not wearing high heels the year before.

110

Reading Comprehension 5

0	High heels are usually associated with …	fashion, fantasy and feminism.
1	Women wearing high heels at work are usually considered …	
2	The country where women are asked to wear high heels at work is …	
3	The idea to collect signatures to stop this practice came to …	
4	She first expressed her disagreement with this practice on …	
5	The English meaning of the words used in the pun coined for the hashtag #KuToo are …	
6	The hashtag #KuToo is especially used by …	
7	Takumi Nemoto maintains that high heels at work are …	
8	In the World Economic Forum's index of gender equality Japan, has a …	

Score: ………. /8

111

Griglie di valutazione

Task di livello B1

Listening Comprehension	Punteggio
Lanzarote is Riding the Wave	.... /7
Uffizi Records	.... /8
Totale	.... /15

Valutazione del livello	
0-5	< B1
6-8	Livello B1 parzialmente raggiunto
9-12	Livello B1 sufficientemente raggiunto
13-15	Livello B1 raggiunto

Reading Comprehension	Punteggio
The International Labour Organization	.... /7
Wimbledon Whites Just Go Green	.... /8
Totale	.... /15

Valutazione del livello	
0-5	< B1
6-8	Livello B1 parzialmente raggiunto
9-12	Livello B1 sufficientemente raggiunto
13-15	Livello B1 raggiunto

Task di livello B2

Listening Comprehension	Punteggio
LA LA Land Reloaded	.... /8
Nicole Kidman	.... /8
The Future of Food	.... /8
Totale	.... /24

Valutazione del livello	
0-10	< B2
10-14	Livello B2 parzialmente raggiunto
15-19	Livello B2 sufficientemente raggiunto
20-24	Livello B2 raggiunto

Reading Comprehension	Punteggio
Hotels in Dublin	.... /8
Bicycle Kingdom	.... /8
Women Say No to High Heels at Work	.... /8
Totale	.... /24

Valutazione del livello	
0-10	< B2
10-14	Livello B2 parzialmente raggiunto
15-19	Livello B2 sufficientemente raggiunto
20-24	Livello B2 raggiunto